Mother
Voices

Mother Voices

Real women
write about
growing into
motherhood

Edited by Traci Dyer

Sourcebooks, Inc.
Naperville, IL

Published by Sourcebooks, Inc.
P.O. Box 372
Naperville, IL 60566
630-961-3900
Fax: 630-961-2168

ISBN 1-887166-45-9

Library of Congress Cataloging-in-Publication Data
Mother voices: real women write about growing into motherhood/edited by
Traci Dyer.
　　　　　p.　　　cm.
　　ISBN 1-887166-45-9 (alk.paper)
　　I.Mothers—Psychology. 2. Motherhood. 3. Mother and child. 4. Women—
Identity. I. Dyer, Traci.
　　HQ759.M8733 1999
　　155.6'463—dc21　　　　　　　　　　　　　　　98-31962
　　　　　　　　　　　　　　　　　　　　　　　　　CIP

Printed and bound in the United States of America
10 9 8 7 6 5 4 3 2 1

Dedication

To my mother, whose example of strength in adversity has helped me to find my own; to my heroes, my daughters, Bree Ashley and Carly Rae, whose courage inspires me; and to mothers everywhere who love their children unconditionally.

Table of Contents

Preface

Traci Dyer
January 27, 1998

Shortly after the birth of my first daughter, Bree Ashley, I began searching bookstores for the writing of other mothers. What I found was disappointing. Plenty of books gave advice on how to raise children, but very few reflected what I was experiencing as a mother trying to adjust to my new identity. In this society, where it's so often "every mother for herself," I was convinced that a book written by mothers in their own words would help me most on my own journey. I wanted to read a book full of mothering experiences, to find my own way through knowing other mothers.

I decided to create what I couldn't find. Through a press release, I invited women to share their stories. In less than a year, I received eight hundred submissions from mothers in thirty states and four countries, the result of which is *Mother Voices.*

I spent the first few years of motherhood resisting the loss of "self." I tried desperately to hold onto a part of me that was separate from my children. However, as I became more adept at achieving that delicate balance, wherein meeting my children's needs supported me in meeting my own and vice versa, I began to stop resisting. As a result, the pages of this book were successfully edited in between diaper changes and late-night breastfeedings.

I started motherhood with a vision of what I thought it would be like, but I've had to adjust along the way. Mothering an infant was very different from mothering a two-year-old. The picture changed again when I became the mother of two, and the most profound change occurred midway through completing this book when I was in a serious car accident with my two daughters. My youngest, Carly

Rae, then just fourteen months old, suffered a traumatic brain injury and was not expected to live.

For two excruciating weeks, my husband, Ralph, and I stood vigil over our daughter in a pediatric intensive care unit. This is when any division left between my identity as an individual and my identity as a mother dissolved and where I fully experienced the solidarity shared by women who are mothers.

Carly continues to exceed every expectation any doctor ever had for her. She has learned how to roll again, much to the delight of her sister. She began saying "Mama" right before Mother's Day last year. She is learning how to sit up and sometimes struggles holding her head. But true to her spirit that has never wavered, these are minor details for Carly. If you help support her head she will show you how she can stand up anyway, laughing and smiling while she waits for Bree to give her what has become known in our house as "Carly's standing up hug." She laughs, she cries, and she pinches Bree. There are so many positive signs for her future.

Working on this book certainly supported me on my own mothering journey, as I hope reading it will do for you. It was reassuring to read how other mothers are managing the stresses and triumphs of this most challenging and rewarding role and comforting to read the words of mothers farther along on the journey.

This book turned out to be much more for me than the "Introduction to Motherhood" I had originally planned, immeasurably more than the professional achievement I sought as a writer and journalist. The courage, tears, and laughter in these pages are the gifts we mothers can offer each other. I hope you find yourself here, and wish you great joy on your mothering journey.

Defining Motherhood

Mothering is a Process

Sheilah Marie Seaberg
St. Paul, Minnesota

Being a mother has been a true learning experience for me. As the fourth of thirteen children, I saw the incredible amount of work it took to be a parent. Now, as mother of three young children (ages eight, four, and two), I know firsthand the tremendous amount of energy the job requires. I also know firsthand the wonder and joy of parenthood. These benefits of parenthood are what I didn't see as a young child observing my own parents. I am certain my parents took joy in us at times, but I was more attuned to the difficulties they encountered.

Motherhood has been a journey of many valuable lessons for me. The more I let go of the idea that I am the sole architect of my own and my childrens' lives, the more I have been able to enjoy the everyday gifts that life as a mother offers.

When my oldest child was born I was like many first-time parents. I had unrealistic expectations of myself as a parent, and therefore, without realizing it, of my child. I frequently felt anxious and at times almost paralyzed by the fear of doing something wrong.

Fortunately, my ideas about the role of a mother have changed a lot in the past eight years. I could never have survived my own perfectionism. Now, I see that mothering, like life, is a process. I don't have to be a perfect parent to help guide my children through life. I can be authentic and human without fearing I am in some way damaging my children. In fact, I believe it's authenticity my kids need to see in order to be comfortable with themselves, and to trust their own instincts and perceptions. My hopes for my children are many, and they are hopes that I believe are shared by all parents in some way.

For Daniel, Stefan, and Moriah, and for all children, I hold these hopes:

May you have healthy self-esteem; may you feel not better than, or less than others, but equally precious; may you feel that you are part of a larger whole, connected to the life around you; may you know and accept yourself and grow to trust your own instincts and perceptions; may you always carry within you a sense of your basic goodness, and the knowledge that it is always okay to ask for help when you need it. May you be at peace with yourselves, so that you will be true peacemakers in our world.

Fifteen Things I Know Now That I Am a Mother

Heather M. Matti
Buffalo, Minnesota

1. Eight hours of sleep is a luxury, not a necessity.
2. Spit is a cleaning fluid.
3. Milk flows from both breasts at the same time (even if you only have one baby).
4. If there's no hair on it after it hits the floor, it's still edible.
5. Even competent parents don't have total control over their children in stores.
6. There are more disgusting things than poop.
7. "Just a minute," "just one more story," and "some assembly required" are all relative terms.
8. My mother was probably once a normal, rational person just like I was.
9. Memory loss and paranoia are not just signs of old age or insanity.
10. You and your husband's bad habits don't get any more endearing when a three-year-old displays them.
11. Kisses really do cure boo-boos.
12. There is an actual instrument at the pediatrician's office just for removing things stuck up a nose.
13. Your husband regresses when your child reaches age two.
14. If a child can choose between stimulating, colorful, educational toys and a dead bug, the child will choose the dead bug.
15. Sitting too close to the television did not make me sterile.

That's my Name

Megan Northland
Miami, Florida

My four-year-old asked me every day one week, "Mommy, what's your name?" "Megan," I told him.

"No!" he retorted. He was not satisfied until I said my first name was Mommy. I tried to explain that to him and his siblings I am Mommy, but to the rest of the world I am Megan Annette Northland. That is who I am, but it is the Mommy part that matters most to my son and the part that comes first for me.

When my four- and five-year-old sons yell "Mommy!" they say it with confidence; faith that there is someone there who cares about their needs. When they say "Mom-eee...," it is often with a bit of disbelief that the bearer of this title could be asking them to do something instead of doing something for them. When my baby says "Mama," it is in a tone of discovery and comfort, knowing that with a simple vocalization she is connected to the center of her universe.

I have seen friends turn into mommies. Women I knew who once swung their arms freely now walk with babies and toddlers. It always startles me when I hear one of these old friends being called "Mommy." To that child, that is unquestionably who my friend is, whether she is in the midst of talking about tax law or changing diapers.

There are so many variations on how to be a mother. Sometimes it seems that as soon as you become one the pressure is to become less of one. To me, statements like: "When are you going back to work?" "Don't hold that baby so much!" "It is so good for their socialization skills when children are in day care," are all attempts to limit my relationship with my children.

However, it matters not whether you spend two or two hundred hours a week with your children, once a child intervenes with "Mommy," all the rest seems trivial. After all, it is the one name you can never change.

$\mathcal{B}$lue T-Shirt

Leslie C. Lacy
East Lansing, Michigan

Where's blue T-shirt?" my daughter asks.

We unroll sleeping bags, shake out backpacks. Apparently "blue T-shirt" is still at the YMCA, forgotten in the rush to pack up after a kids' overnight party.

I sigh, exchange my slippers for shoes (it's still relatively early on this Saturday morning), grab the keys and head for the Y. Once there, I quickly find blue T-shirt in the lost-and-found box, along with the forgotten belongings of other happy, tired children.

I thank the girl behind the desk. "My daughter can't sleep without blue T-shirt." She laughs and says, "That's odd."

"It's a long story," I reply on my way out the door.

Go back five years. Laurie nursed to go to sleep; then a middle-of-the night session if she woke up. It worked for her older sister, Katie. She nursed until she was ready to wean and tapered off so gradually that I can't remember when and how she stopped.

Not true of Laurie. She stopped nursing at 3 A.M. on October 10. My happy, agreeable baby, so predictable until that night, woke up fussing. When I sat down to nurse her, as usual, she looked blankly at my proffered breast as if she'd never seen it before. Then she firmly turned her head away as though to tell me that if I wanted to mash that thing in her ear it was my business, but we'd both look awfully silly.

I was baffled. I had two problems now. My immediate problem was one of overproduction. Over the next week, I came to identify with every dairy cow who has ever had to wait, udder full to bursting, for the farmer to come milk her. My other problem was a fussy child who was rejecting the go-to-sleep solution that had always worked before.

Reasoning that maybe a reminder of Mom, something with Mom's scent and feel to it, might help Laurie go back to sleep, I slipped off the T-shirt I was wearing and gave it to her to snuggle. It was nothing special; a blue, medium-sized T-shirt, with a facsimile of Salvador Dali's autograph dashed across the front that my husband had bought at a museum gift shop while on a business trip.

Laurie melted into sleep like one of Dali's surreal watches, and blue T-shirt has been her nighttime companion ever since.

So I suppose the girl behind the desk and I were both wrong. It isn't such a long story after all, but neither is it odd. So many of the objects precious to us seem unremarkable to the outsider. Only we know how special they are; how circumstances and memories made them so.

hocolate Milk

Maureen Sklaroff
Redmond, Washington

Rivulets run down the table, down the chair, and onto the floor, spreading and growing like the Blob from those old horror movies. Something inside me gives as the brown puddle stills, the fluorescent lights flickering off its surface. I lose it. No other phrase describes it. I've had it.

Oh, this day. This long, dreary day. I cannot endure even one more thing. The things I've endured already. The tantrums. The never ending stream of tantrums this day has thrown at me. Tantrums over this, tantrums over that. Tantrums over dressing, eating, drinking, bathing, breathing, sleeping, leaving, coming, sitting, and standing.

And the messes. I've cleaned markers off the walls, mud off the carpets, peanut butter off the furniture. I've read, played, counted, spelled, showed, negotiated, cooked, cleaned, laundered, and bathed throughout this long day. Through it all, I've remained patient (fairly so, anyway).

But chocolate milk. Chocolate milk everywhere I turn. On the floor, on her dress, on the table, on my shoes. As my body stiffens, the only movement is my blood flowing swiftly through my veins, filling my head with its dreadful rhythmic pounding that makes it hard to hear anything else.

I cannot tear my eyes away from this puddle of vile, mutated dairy product. I smell nothing but sickly sweet cocoa and milk, and I taste my anger. Suddenly I'm yelling, and I hold nothing back. My yell reverberates frustration and fatigue. How can one person be expected to endure so much? I am only human. Doesn't she understand that? Why can't she give me five minutes of solitude and peace?

As I notice another cry meshing with my own, I am able to look beyond this odoriferous puddle of moo juice and I see this tiny person, weeping, eyes cast downward. I feel my cheeks burn in shame, for I have failed, I am fallible. Every day I must see just how much so, for motherhood is the ultimate test.

I sigh loudly, and reach to give her a hug. I am overwhelmed with love, for there is no reproach in her eyes, no questioning of my actions, no judgment. Her hug is full and warm, and gets chocolate milk all over my new white shirt, but I don't care. The chill is overcome by the warmth of her love.

A Search for Balance

Carol T. Jacobson
Minneapolis, Minnesota

I am one of the lucky ones. One son, one daughter. Two deliveries, both earlier than expected. One by C-section, the other by Northwest Airlines.

There was our son, not gaining weight for the first three weeks of his life, but soon on the fast track. And our daughter, born much tinier, nine miniature pounds at four months of age. Off the bottom of the growth charts. "We've seen newborns bigger," the doctors said.

Being a mother is definitely all about tiny fingers and nursing mouths, and firsts. First smiles, first rolls, first steps, first words, and first days of school. It is loving dreams and expectations. Motherhood also is what happens when the doctor says, "Let's talk about cerebral palsy."

Her smile made her such a gorgeous baby. We were putty in her hands, obviously, but total strangers also were easily charmed by her high-voltage smile. Her smile carried her through countless waiting rooms, visits to rehabilitative doctors, speech, occupational and physical therapists, pediatric neurologists, opthalmologists, audiologists, makers of therapeutic devices, and everyone who wanted to reach out and touch, manipulate and feel for themselves. Why not smile at everyone? Wasn't this simply life? Doesn't everyone experience all this?

Motherhood is all the reading, the theories, the exercises and the recommendations. It is refusing to believe it when someone of authority and experience says, "She will never run. She will never skip. She will never ride a bike." It is incredible joy and gratitude when, at eight, she does all of those things. Awkwardly, but smiling, with the wind blowing through her hair.

Parenting is a search for balance. Do I encourage her to try what she might be incapable of doing? It is considering the needs of the well child, too, who spends hours in waiting rooms, but goes unnoticed in the exams and questions and fuss.

Cerebral palsy used to be just physical things; physical things we could "fix," but one day she came home and her smile had dimmed. The teasing had begun. "She shakes. We won't be her friend because she shakes." Who, but a mother, lies awake at night feeling her daughter's pain? She is furious now and at eight years old says, "I won't be different."

The hardest thing about motherhood is not knowing what the final outcome is actually going to be. The results, your mature son, your mature daughter, are years down the road. Every day is an effort. Hope, love, and responsibility keep you going. I find that I cannot separate my well-being from the well-being of my children, at least not yet. They are in me, they are me.

He's into preadolescent moodiness, she has never needed so much energy for her emotional well-being. They like school. They have friends. They behave well. Adults like them. We have fun together. We are a family, a strong family. They are special, unique people.

Motherhood is not what I expected. Motherhood is a challenge. It is a mystery. It is exhausting and it is rewarding. It doesn't come with guarantees, directions, or a rule book. It is different for every mother, and different as we consider each individual child.

"Mom" is such a simple, short word, but there are only two people on Earth who call me that. For them, home is where Mom is, and it is the safest and best place to be. The relationships and responsibilities are awesome. Their father is great, and so are they. We've worked hard to define home and family and we all like the results.

Motherhood has challenged me and changed me. Sometimes it feels overwhelming. I get lonely, I get angry, yet I can't imagine life without it. It's the most adventurous path I have ever taken.

New to Winter

Linda Kelly-Hassett
Longmont, Colorado

As the darkish day was ending and our good friends were leaving, giant glistening snowflakes began weaving their way to the ground. My toddler stood in awe at the sight. She reached out to touch a few snowflakes and was surprised at how quickly they melted in her hand. She ran to the window for another look when the door shut out the cold night.

The light of the porch lamp reached far across the yard and illuminated the snowflakes that continued to fall, each one seeming to grow in size as it entered the light. My daughter turned to me, smiled, pointed up, and actually said, "Sky." I was delighted and scooped her up. We sat by the window watching the swirling snowflakes swishing through the air. She suddenly jumped from the chair and pulled me toward the stairs. She pointed to a picture of snow-dressed alpine trees. She was sharing her new-found understanding.

Winter at the window, on the wall a snowy view, back and forth she ran, the connection she made was so new. The snow outside became entwined with the picture on the paper. We sat and read *The Snowman* together. She clapped and trembled with delight.

A magical thing happened to this mother and her new-to-winter toddler that night. It is the kind of evening I know will never fade from my memory, and it never has.

*L*ois

Mary Mitchell Lundeen
Elk River, Minnesota

"Lois, I need more Cheerios," is a statement I hear every morning. But Lois is not my name—not my first name, not my last name. Nevertheless, "Lois" is what I have been called for the past year.

I am Lois, as in Superman's not-so-observant friend and Clark Kent's overly competent colleague. My two young sons have been Supermen all year. There is hardly anything more endearing or enlightening than this preschool age of pretending, so please call me Lois.

Lois has discovered through motherhood that Supermen can come in all ages. In my house, one is four years old, one is five, and one is forty-one years old. The oldest one comes with a unique set of superhero qualities. He has supersonic hearing, a finely tuned internal clock, and an extra-perceptive sensory system. Translated in human terms, he gets up with the kids at night, comes home on time from work every day, and heats up the boys' robes in the dryer during baths. All of this makes Lois fall more deeply in love with him, with or without his cape.

Lois also knows that mankind is meant to be good. The oldest Superman and I are teaching spiritual thought at home—interwoven in interactions and experiences. As preschoolers, our boys rarely need discipline. Through repeated exposure, they have the beginnings of the life philosophy we want them to live by.

They know that family comes first, that people are to be treated with dignity, that rules have reasons behind them, and that God lies within oneself.

No kryptonite needed here. These little superheroes have developed their powers and can apply them at will.

During the past year I have learned to love the name Lois and understand the lessons shown to me.

Ordinary Blessings

Kerin McTeigue O'Connor
St. Paul, Minnesota

In my dream, I am rummaging through drawers and boxes for treasures in Grandma's attic when crying from the next room brings me back to the present. I slip out of bed to get Luke. In the darkness of his room, I smell that he has thrown up. Still half asleep, I pull the sheets off his bed and resist the urge to retch, which still comes over me after three kids. In my mind I have already begun rearranging my expectations for the day ahead. I will have to cancel my walking date with Linnea. Forget the parent-child group at my church. No nursery school for Luke. No writing at the café for me. I get Luke comfortable and I return for some more sleep.

In the morning, I am exhausted after having gotten up a few more times during the night. As Patrick and the older kids leave for work and school I wipe dried egg and raspberry jam off the kitchen counters and wonder what to do next. Luke is still asleep.

"Maybe you can get some writing done while he naps," my husband said as he kissed me goodbye, knowing I was disappointed to be missing my time at the café.

I fixed myself another cup of coffee and tightened the belt around my sea-green bathrobe before sitting down in the big easy chair in the corner of the kitchen. With my notebook on my lap, I unscrew my fountain pen and begin writing. I recreate Grandma's attic: the boxes, the old jewelry and the '30s skirt and jacket I tried on in my dream last night. Then I remembered I discovered her mandolin.

In real life, we'd begged Grandma to play that mandolin after we found it in a dusty leather case behind the dressmaker's form in the corner of the attic.

"Oh, I haven't played in years," she said, slim and elegant in her lavender silk blouse and heels as she stood above my cousins and me. She was quiet for a moment as she turned the mandolin in her hands.

"We don't care if you're out of tune," we persisted, but she silenced us by banishing us from the attic and vaguely promising, the way grown-ups do to children when they want to get them out of their hair, that, "maybe someday..."

In the dream, I tell her how mad I was after that. I was too afraid to tell her back then. She was so reserved and formal.

"My tummy hurts, Mom," Luke moans, suddenly standing next to my chair. I didn't hear him coming. His light brown hair is tousled and sticking up. His face is pale against the red long underwear I changed him into in the middle of the night. I put my notebook down on the floor as he climbs onto my lap and creates a little nest for himself within the circle of my arms. We sit this way for a while and then drift off. The music from the radio and the commentator's smooth voice are soothing and far away.

Luke shifts in my lap and I notice the clock on the microwave. It's only 9:43 A.M. when I decide to call my sister Margaret in New York, just for the treat of talking to an adult. I'm confident she'll be home since she just had her first baby three weeks ago.

"It's unbelievable. I can't get anything done," she tells me. "I mean, it's an accomplishment if I get dressed by noon."

"Get used to it," I tell her, looking down at Luke on my lap. I have this defeated feeling at the moment as I think about the day ahead of me.

"It's the name of the game," I continue, not even caring that I am breaking one of my own rules. When our kids were babies, older mothers would come up to me and say, "Enjoy them now." They lifted their voice up at the "now," insinuating that they knew things I didn't. This of course, was true, but didn't stop me from swearing that I would never talk that way to a new mom.

Before becoming a mother, I swore I'd never let my life be dominated by my children so much that I'd lose track of myself and things I loved doing, the way Grandma forgot the feel of the mandolin in her hands and the music she could make with it.

"I'm hungry, Mom," Luke whines. He is getting louder and I realize I need to get off the phone.

"Hang in there," Margaret and I encourage each other in farewell.

"You can have something to drink, but not to eat yet," I tell Luke and get up to get him a glass of the Gatorade we keep for just such occasions. I pour the lime green liquid into a mango-colored Tupperware cup and look away as he downs it. I can't stand the stuff, but to our kids it's one of the treats of being sick.

"I'm hungry!" Luke repeats, shouting and turning his words into a war cry as he follows me from the sink to the refrigerator.

I feel like I am being hunted and I pick up my pace so he can't catch me. He reaches out to grab the end of my bathrobe. I step just out of his reach and he collapses in tears on the kitchen floor.

"Mean mother," I say to myself, scooping him up in my arms. "It's okay, it's okay," I tell him with a sudden rush of understanding for both of us. I sway back and forth with him in my arms.

When I lay my cheek against his it feels hot. "You need some medicine," I tell him, and I put him down on the cushioned bench so I can reach the cabinet above the sink.

"Come on," I coax him, putting the spoonful of red liquid to his lips. He takes his thumb out of his mouth just long enough to swallow it and then lies down and closes his eyes.

"Perfect time for me to run upstairs and get dressed," I say to myself. As I pass the bathroom, I see the slump of sheets I left in the bathtub last night, too tired to lug them down the washer after finally getting Luke cleaned up and

settled down. Into the laundry basket they go, which I start to carry downstairs when Cappuccino, our dog, charges the front door, barking wildly.

Luke wakes up wailing in the kitchen. I put the laundry basket down on the living room floor. That was the mailman and I realize that means it is noon already and I am still in my pajamas. Luke is screaming. I resist the impulse to join him.

Much later, after the other children have come home from school and are outside playing, Luke falls asleep lying beside me on the cushioned bench at the kitchen table. I have been carrying around my notebook and fountain pen hoping that I might get a minute to write.

Taking time for myself, and writing in particular, puts me in touch with something much greater than myself. It allows me to step back from the daily picking up of socks, helping with homework, and figuring out whose night it is to do dishes and to see the bigger picture. It is what makes me want to sink my face deep into the colorful bouquet of ordinary moments that make up my life, to smell the bitter and the sweet, and to know them all as blessings.

So even on the days when I don't get the break I planned for, I can savor the way the late afternoon light filters through the green leaves of the oak tree in the backyard, and not mind so much that my time is over because Luke just woke up from his nap, red-cheeked and crying.

I pick up Luke and I kiss his sweaty forehead, pressing my nose into his damp hair and breathe in his three-year-old scent. I want to be in this moment, and I let my writing go for now. I hold Luke in my arms, enjoying the weight of his body in my lap, his head against my breasts. We lean back together against a cushion and watch the shadows of leaves flicker across the kitchen table. Through the open window beside me I hear the trees rustling in the breeze and the kids playing outside. And in the distance I hear the music of my grandmother's mandolin.

Siesta Bliss

Penny Reid
Seattle, Washington

We might as well post a "We nap here. Disturb at your own risk" sign in our front yard. In essence, that's what the small, polite "Please knock" taped to our doorbell means. With my first child, as soon as he fell asleep I was haunted by a need to "hop-to" during his nap time. The long list of tasks that could be accomplished without a toddler (or any age child, for that matter) underfoot was daunting, and I spent my share of early afternoon hours flying around the house like a beheaded chicken. Somehow, the sense of accomplishment never quite outweighed the exhaustion I felt ten minutes after my son was up and at it full-speed-ahead again. I persevered for a while, knowing that every now and then the conversation about what-I-managed-to-produce-during-naptime would come up with some other mother. Thankfully, my husband stayed well away from any such topics. He simply counted his blessings if there was milk for his morning cereal and clean underwear in the dryer.

So here I am, many years later, realizing that I can probably only count on a few more months of regular napping, and I am dreading it. I know that some moms looked forward to uninterrupted days when planning around naptime is no longer necessary. Let it be said, though, that I am not one of those. In fact, I have discovered my true biological clock, thanks to this business of mothering. Yes, I am both early bird and night owl, given a good stretch of siesta bliss in between. And I don't mean a catnap either. Two hours defines "siesta" in my book, and it's blissful if I can sleep beside my three-year-old daughter and begin waking up, oh say, fifteen minutes before she does. Ah yes, ecstasy.

See, we were blessed with a little girl who truly knows how to cuddle. She has taught each of us the joy of an uninterrupted snuggle, and we snatch extra curl-ups whenever possible. Our naps usually begin with what we call "a good read." Her after-lunch comment, "Let's have a good read, Mommy," signals the slowdown to siesta time. I always disconnect the phone at this point and lock all the doors. Any interruption is such a disappointment. It used to be that Carolina's next signal, after we'd stretched out together, was sucking her thumb and twirling her hair. This habit recently took on a delightful twist, as my daughter popped her thumb in her mouth and reached for my hair. With this kind of treatment I usually slip away before she does, waking refreshed. On the best days, I stretch and yawn like a cat, marveling all the while that I feel so nurtured by this little one beside me.

Of course, lest you think ours is the only home in the world where one can count on such pure, peaceful ritual day after day, some days are different. We pick up Clarke at three o'clock "sharp" (that expression is a joke after becoming a parent) on school days. We both really look forward to his return, so even when we settle in for a late nap, we can handle the radio alarm if it's classical music. Things get turned around, too, if one or the other of us is sick, or if Rob gets off early, or (and this is the worst) if Carolina falls asleep in her car seat. Blast…the old illusion of a full snooze after a brief seven-and-a-half minute doze under the influence of movement. I kiss siesta bliss good-bye on those days.

This schedule suits me. With a nap under my belt, I can conquer the world, so to speak. (But who would want to?) I am rested and ready for the most demanding and rewarding hours of my day: afternoon snack and playtime, just-before-dinner "arsenic hour," dinner, homework, stories, baths, etc. And, amazingly, there's even energy left after the kids are in bed. I've been known to mop the floor, albeit infrequently, after hours; or to curl up with a good book; or, believe it or not, to curl up with my husband for more than the flop-into-bed-from-sheer-exhaustion routine. Then, on the other side of the day, I can usually wake early, before everyone else, for my own quiet study time. It works because over time I realized that this stretch of regular midday downtime won't last forever. I choose to savor it knowing that my child's own rhythm is best for her growth and nurture, and probably downright healthy for me, too.

$\mathcal{B}$eing Home

Sara Jane Burant
Eugene, Oregon

A thick, overnight frost has settled on rooftops and cars like dust in an unoccupied house—or in a busy occupied one. I scan bookshelves and tabletops heaped with paper airplanes, birds, and sea mammals made from folded origami paper, letters to and from grandparents and pen pals, dictionaries, currently favorite read-alouds, coins and stamps and various puzzle pieces, notebooks, journals, whichever encyclopedias hold information on the latest topics of interest: Australian marsupials, dinosaurs, kings and queens of Britain, snakes, weaponry. The harum-scarum scholars who have accumulated the lion's share of this heap are not at the moment poring over their texts and papers. My sons, the scholars, are where they usually are at this hour—outside.

Elated by the frost, they dashed out of the house mittenless and hatless but ready for anything, to meet the sun's first shower of rays over the hill to the east of our house. Their first "find" of the morning is a thin glaze of ice on our experimental pond, murky water in a plastic tub inside of an old barrel, awaiting occupants in the warmer days ahead. They have broken off slabs of ice in varying sizes and carry them as gingerly as they would great-grandmother's crystal. They put them in the freezer for future use.

Having donned gloves and hats, they are now scraping frost from the car and elsewhere, piling it up, skidding through it. I listen to their shouts and laughter. I smile. Countless mornings, throughout the past three years, my smile might have been rueful or bittersweet. I might have been wondering how I was going to get them to come inside and get to work on math problems or spelling. This morning

24   ～ *Mother Voices* ～

my conviction is strong, as theirs has always been, that they are at work. They are learning the weather, absorbing the signs of early spring. They are experiencing how a frosty morning in early March is different from a frosty morning in December. The texture of this particular March morning is weaving itself into the tapestry of their lives. Some parents, more assiduous than I, might call this early morning outing Science and Nature Studies. I shirk such labels. My sons don't go to school, nor do they have school at home.

Stomping feet on the deck announces their approach. My nine-year-old son, Geoffrey, rushes in with a draft of cold air. He heads directly for the workbench, a boy with a mission. The cold air chases away my musings, stirs my curiosity.

"What's up?" I ask.

"Well, we're fixing something."

"Hmmm. What're you fixing?"

"Well, the mailboxes. You know how they're bent backwards. We're bending them forward and propping them up against a piece of wood."

"Sounds great."

"Only a board broke. We're replacing it. That's why I need nails."

"Did you find some?"

"Yeah," he says jingling the nails in his pockets and dashing out the door.

Our mailbox and those of our two neighbors are fastened onto a board which is in turn fastened onto a post. For months, the post has wobbled like a punching bag, probably making the mail carrier feel like he wanted to punch us for not fixing it. For a while the hammers whack and pound the board, the nailheads. Then I am called upon to examine their work. Holding my sweater tightly around me, I observe that the warmth of the climbing sun has already soaked up most of the frost from the surrounding rooftops. The tiny unfurling leaves of the lilac gleam as though they were waxed by that same sweep of sunlight. The post stands straight and tall once more.

The boys have done important work this morning. They identified something that needed fixing. They assessed what needed to be done. They collected materials for the job and executed the task they set for themselves. The completed project benefits our neighbors, the mail carrier, and our family.

Three years ago, we dove into home-schooling without really knowing what we were getting into. I'd read a few books and several articles about it written both by parents who were engaged in home-schooling their children, and by advocates who weren't parents but had been educators. Still, as with parenting in general, I have charted my own course and at times been kept afloat by the support I've found in books and articles, from my best friend whose children attend school, from the stranger I meet now and then who truly sees me, my husband, the children, and our family.

The decision itself, to keep the boys home from school, was an easy one. We were not happy with the private school Geoffrey was attending for kindergarten. His bold, independent nature never fit the mold formed by the school's overreaching ideology. It broke my heart to watch the teachers try to squeeze him in. I passively assumed they must be right; he could fit if only this adjustment was made, or that. In retrospect, our decision to take charge seems to have come quite suddenly. I knew it could never work, he would never fit, and I loved him all the more because of it.

Next, I explored the many options our community offers within the public school system. Not only do the schools have open enrollment, but there are also several "alternative" schools, each of which offers a unique approach to education, from the teaching of foreign languages, to curriculum intensive in the arts, to schools that focus on communication and leadership skills. My son's name wasn't chosen in the lottery for any of those schools. That left the regular schools, and they seemed, well, just too regular. I didn't think my children would be honored, day in and day out, as the unique individuals they are in classrooms where one teacher is in charge of twenty-five or more children, each one of whom has his or her own needs and interests that deserve to be acknowledged.

Only recently have I begun to feel the weight of that decision that once seemed so easy to make. The weight is not a burden, and because of it I have been able to shed certain ideas and expectations that lighten my load considerably. I have learned to let go of the notion that there are certain subjects every child must be taught, that there are particular ways in which children must be taught the elements of those subjects, and that there is an order in which they must be taught. These notions serve to compartmentalize reality and to remove education from experience. Education, i.e. learning, happens all the time. I have watched the boys learn the fundamentals of arithmetic through earning money and buying things, by baking or simply asking the questions they love to ask. How many millions make a billion? How many seconds are in a minute, an hour, a day, a year? How many miles are in a light-year? How much taller is the Empire State Building than the Statue of Liberty? Geoffrey learned to read not through workbooks, phonics drills, or methodology, but through hearing me read aloud a lot, deciding he wanted to read, asking myriad questions and putting it all together by reading books he found interesting and worthwhile.

Once I let go of the belief that only school offers the kind of learning opportunities that really matter, I discovered a wellspring of trust in my children and respect for their choices. I trust that they are doing what they need to do, that they are learning what they need to learn during every moment of every day, whether they are daydreaming, practicing the piano, playing with friends, bouncing a basketball in the driveway, or looking at and reading books.

However, I feel the weight of our decision to home-school in the questions that sometimes haunt me. Do my children and I spend too much time together? Am I seeing clearly or have I talked myself into believing radical ideas, the practice of which is, at best, experimental? Is there a right path? Are we following it? I must learn to trust myself the way I have learned to trust my children.

My younger son, Erik, and I are engaged in a friendly game of chess. We are fairly evenly matched. He often plays with a reckless, disarming acuity, but today his attention wanders, and he has lost a number of his key players in this chess-board drama. His older brother's attention drifts in our direction. Assuming that his help is not only needed but desired, Geoffrey comes to the table armed with a strategy he believes in: protect your king, but for God's sake preserve the queen! He starts making moves for Erik who wavers between welcoming and shunning the unsolicited assistance. I achieve checkmate. The situation rapidly deteriorates.

With tears and wailing, Erik blames Geoffrey for losing the game for him. Sheepish but unrepentant, Geoffrey goes on the defensive. Ugly things are said. I am unsure of how to positively impact the rising conflict. Tired of the verbal sparring, in which they are equals, Geoffrey decides to dominate with a blow to Erik's shoulder.

I swing into action, ordering Geoffrey to take a timeout. It provides us all with a few minutes to cool off.

Almost as soon as the timeout is over, the boys are giggling together over something or other, the chess game all but forgotten. It takes me longer to recover my equanimity.

I continue to reflect. Do I accept the intermittent, yet emotionally charged conflicts as just part of it all, the inevitable result of brothers spending so much time in each other's company? After all, they do spend a lot of time together and so have a unique interdependence of interests and activities and even behavior and moods. Yet, even when I manage to keep my distance, even when I acknowledge their ownership of the conflict, their conflicts have an impact on my life and often leave me emotionally exhausted.

What, then, is my role when their coping skills disintegrate? In the particular context of the chess match and conflict, should I have taken the initiative through an exploration of feelings? Did Geoffrey's interference in the game stem in part from a desire to be interacting with us? Did he feel left out? I'll never know; I didn't ask. Was Erik feeling less than confident about his own ability? Geoffrey's interference was a tacit statement that Erik doesn't play well enough on his own, and I had to make matters worse by winning. Again, I'll never know for sure. Clearly I missed an opportunity to ask questions, to bring issues out in the open, to air grievances. Given the chance, Erik will not hesitate to talk about how he feels. One astute question or observation opens his floodgates. Geoffrey is more reticent, less willing or able to verbally express how he feels. Still, the right question can bring out a trickle. While it rarely turns into a flood, it can clearly indicate the direction of the flow.

In an appropriately querulous tone, I ask myself why it can't be simpler. I think of the mornings I have trouble getting out of bed. How I pull the covers over my head, hoping that if I stay there long enough the boys will disappear to well-ordered classrooms where somebody else is in charge. It is then that I remind myself that the geography we are learning is as much that of the inner landscape of feelings and communication as that of mountain ranges and seaports. In school, the geography of the interior self is left largely unexplored. There just isn't time. We, on the other hand, have all the time in the world to explore what is important.

At a nearby department store, I am absent-mindedly eyeing items on the sale table. Is that what women do when they do not have their children in tow nearly everywhere they go? I am not, however, alone. Erik's attention is held by a Disney video playing in the children's department not ten feet away. But I can pretend.

"Are you really alone?"

Startled, I turn. It's my neighbor, Laurie. I guess I must have looked the part.

"No. Erik's over there watching a video," I say pointing to the children's department.

"It looked like you were having some time to yourself."

"Not today."

"You poor woman. Do you ever get time to yourself?"

I make stammered assurances that I do. We exchange neighborly pleasantries, then she departs to make her purchase. I linger over racks of adorable baby clothes I no longer need. Laurie is also a mother of two and teaches part-time at a middle school. She has one child in first grade, the other goes to day care until

3:30 P.M. Her lithe, slender form attests to her passion for fitness. It isn't surprising, then, that perhaps she views my life as somewhat hemmed in. For a moment I imagine that if my kids were in school I might regain the willowy form of my early twenties—Laurie's form. (Nah. I'd spend my time obsessing about cleaning and reading bestsellers.)

I make my purchase, collect Erik, and dash off to pick up Geoffrey from his piano teacher's house, feeling both validated and misunderstood.

What does it mean to be a mother at home with her school-age children who are not going to school? How do I define myself? The comments I hear most often from people who don't know me very well have to do with the saintly reserves of patience I must possess. While I must admit that being put on a pedestal comes with a fleeting sense of satisfaction, I must also confess that any measure of patience I possess beyond the reserves of the average mom comes not from kinship with the saints but from our relaxed and flexible schedule. Give me a time card to punch at 9:00 A.M., lunch-making to monitor, two children to see off to the school bus, errands to run on my lunch hour, four separate schedules to keep track of, etc., and no one would think of me as patient.

I cringe at the thought of being considered saintly, sacrificing my life for the sake of my children. Whether or not they agree with our choice to home-school, most people seem to think the children benefit from it and that I, as the parent at home, am running a reasonable facsimile of school at home. I am not a teacher. In relation to my children I think of myself as a facilitator. I encourage exploration and discovery; I discuss ideas with them and answer heaps of questions, as often as not with more questions; I look for opportunities for them to develop their interests through classes, "field trips," participation in sports and other groups; I support who they are and where they're at. I am their advocate, their friend, and still, under all circumstances, their mother.

Beyond this, the image I have of myself often becomes fuzzy. There are days that don't seem complete without reading aloud to the boys for an hour or two or having one of their activities around which to organize my day. Yet, I am learning to create and sustain a self-image that moves beyond, yet includes and honors, the stay-at-home mom of two home-schooled children. Sometimes, with grand sweeping gestures and sometimes with minuscule rearrangements, I have cleared space for myself, space in which I see myself as writer, gardener, chef, political activist, volleyball player, and lifelong learner.

I think about what it takes to survive as a stay-at-home mom, about the kind of space, mental and physical, I crave from time to time, space where I am separate from my family while holding family at the center of my life. Having a career, or at least an income-producing job, has become the norm for women. The women's movement gave me the power to choose from a range of possibilities of which my mother never could have conceived. Though my choices seem to have left me spinning in the backwater, I am as much a part of the movement as the other mothers in our neighborhood, all of whom have careers or jobs outside the home. Within the circle defined by my choice, there is a spiral of endless possibilities which begins and ends with my home-schooling family.

I am collecting the mail from the newly straight and tall mailbox and pause to chat with my neighbor. Diane has four children between the ages of eleven and seventeen. We engage in the usual mailbox chatter until Diane tells me where she has just been—at the funeral of a twenty-two-year-old young man who died in an auto accident over spring break.

"You have to take time to be with them," she says. "You have to really look at them, into their eyes, at who they are because you just never know."

Maybe this is the reason above all other reasons. We are home together because you just never know. Each moment seems like a single grain of sand on a wide beach, yet we only own one grain of sand at a time. And whatever else my life is about, I have spent time with my children. I know them and I release them.

Make a Pathway

Carolyn H. Connor
Utica, Michigan

My children come by their "pack ratness" honestly. Grandpa is a child of the Great Depression. Anyone with a family member who lived through this troubled era needs no further explanation than that. My parents also have lived at the same address for thirty-seven years. Their place is truly awesome. Not in the, "my soul has been touched" kind of awesome, but rather the, "I can't believe my eyes" kind.

Dad has reached the point of not being able to find anything anymore; he just knows, "It's someplace around here." And Mom's closet looks as though she's trying to hide some secret passageway to a roomful of treasures. Their basement, garage, and several other expanding sheds are filled beyond standing room only. Both blame the other for the stockpile, both are equally guilty.

The reality of all of this came to my attention while trying to figure out how to store my children's possessions. I'm really gifted in the organization department but their rooms are outside any form of hope. The closets, underneath furniture, shelves, and drawers are groaning like someone's stomach after Thanksgiving dinner. And my kids keep stuffing more into those rooms like forcing dessert down after that meal.

My two children will do anything within their power to keep me out of their rooms. Fearing the worst—me and a thirty-gallon garbage bag—they scurry to neaten up piles if I even mention spring or fall cleaning. Truth be known, I really don't want to know what is hidden from my eyes. I don't worry because there is no doubt in my mind that they are not harboring contraband of any sort. There's no room for cigarettes, dope, or booze. But I might question why they have a

shoebox full of rocks ("They're my fossil collection, Mom!") or what's with the pile of two-year-old magazines ("reference material!") and why can't we get rid of all these little toys from fast-food "fun meals."

But like their grandparents, I know that these things represent a type of security to them. I do think that as parents, it is our main responsibility to insure that our children grow up with a strong sense of security. Sometimes that isn't an easy task. My two are like so many children of our times, victims of divorce. When I remarried, I gave up a good job that I loved in order to be at home for them, for their sense of security. I figured they had had enough upheaval with the divorce and eventually a new home, school, and Dad. I decided what they needed was a constant, and that was me.

I won't force them to scale down too much. I'll let them hang onto their bits and pieces of security, the things that let them know we'll be here tomorrow and the day after. And in deciding to do so, I have just one small request of them: please, for the safety of others and myself who might dare to venture into your minefields, make a pathway.

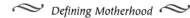

Trying for a Girl?

Melanie Rome
Tarzana, California

People who don't know me keep asking the same question.

"Are you gonna try for a girl?"

You see, I have three sons. My youngest was born just a couple of months ago, and despite what some people might think, I couldn't be happier.

For most of my life I've wanted three children. My dream has come true. I don't care that they are all the same gender, and boys at that. It's just that other people think that I wanted one of them to be a girl, especially the last one.

Perhaps my lack of preference was colored by perspective. In the process of having my three sons, I had two miscarriages, one after my oldest son and one before my youngest. So when I prayed to God each time we tried to conceive it was for a healthy baby without regard to gender. Besides, if there is any truth to it, genetics were in favor of us having boys. Out of the last twenty-two births on my husband's side of the family, nineteen are boys.

A large gap (ten years) exists between my middle and youngest child. Some people assume I was making a last-ditch effort to have a girl. That's not true. It just took me eight years to convince my husband to have another child. He's happy with our decision now; he just needed some coaxing. Trust me, no one can resist the adorable face of our third son.

I'd like to dispel a few myths about being the mother of three boys.

Three boys. How boring. Well, not to me. I see each of our children as individuals. They look, act, and think differently. Each phase of their development has been unique. My oldest slept through the night at six weeks, my middle son at two years (I was beginning to wonder if he ever would) and my youngest at two months. They all have distinct preferences. My oldest loves to challenge his mind and my middle son challenges his coordination with basketball. One's a budding scientist, the other a "people person." We're still waiting on number three. Right now he's fascinated with his crib mobile that dangles Disney characters above his head.

I'll never have the fun of dressing a girl. Children's clothing has changed. Boys don't dress only in blue, black, or brown. Designers now incorporate into boys' styles pink, purple, and other colors previously considered "only for girls." My middle son is fashion-conscious and picky about what he wears despite the fact that he is "all boy." And nothing can compare to the joy I experienced helping my oldest son pick out his navy blue double-breasted suit and turquoise tie for his bar mitzvah.

I can't do "girl stuff" with boys. Activities for girls only? Not these days. My oldest son, at thirteen, loves to "do lunch" and window-shop at the mall. True, he might not be interested in looking at the same things I am, but he is a fun person to hang out with.

How about gossiping? In my family, gossiping is not restricted to women. My ten-year-old loves to pass along tidbits of information about his friends and their families. He's even proven to be a reliable source.

It must be hard being the only girl in the house. I like being the only rose amongst the ferns. There is no competition. Nor does my house smell or resemble a boys' locker room. I haven't gone hog wild in the other direction either, and I have no desire to paint the living room pink.

Nothing can replace the mother-daughter relationship. My only rebuttal for that myth is that nothing compares with the relationship I have with my sons. I want to protect them, watch them mature, and it's my privilege to indulge them.

So when people ask me if I'm going to have any more children, I give them my stock answer, "When I win the lottery."

The truth is, I already feel like I've won.

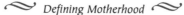 *Defining Motherhood*

ear Mary

Lana Stone
Stillwater, Oklahoma

I talked with your friend, Joan, today, and she told me that you are having a difficult time since you found out that your daughter is gay. Although we haven't met and I don't even know your last name, I wanted to offer you some support. It was just a year ago that I found out my oldest son is gay.

It came as quite a shock. Although he had never shown much interest in girls or in dating throughout high school and college, he never gave me any reason to suspect that he was anything other than heterosexual. Indeed, the discovery of his sexuality at age twenty-three surprised even him. He told me he had "mulled over the possibility that he might be gay" for a year-and-a-half before beginning his first relationship.

If you are at all the way I was, you are probably experiencing a confusing array of emotions right now, everything ranging from feelings of loss and sadness to anger, self-doubt, and guilt. The feelings have a way of tumbling together and it is hard to sort them out.

I still remember the numbness and disbelief I felt when my son made his initial pronouncement over the phone that evening in March. "I think I might be gay," he said gently, almost apologetically.

Shaken and struggling for words, my response came straight from the heart: "I love you, K.C., more than anything. Nothing could ever change that."

"Thank you," he said softly, his voice filled with gratitude and relief.

As I hung up the phone, I remember feeling the presence of a big, dark cloud overhead. It was ominous and oppressive, a private sense of sadness, and I felt that it would always be with me and that life would never be the same. How could it be, living with the threat of AIDS and the risk of an untimely death for my son? I feared for my son's safety, for his happiness and well-being. Could he live the fulfilling, productive life I wanted for him as a gay person in our homophobic society? Would he have to remain in the closet to avoid discrimination and bashing?

Over the next few months, I grieved the loss of the dreams that I once had for my son—dreams of a spouse and children, of a white picket fence and the life I thought he would lead. I grieved the wedding I'd never attend, the daughter-in-law I would never meet, and most of all, holiday reunions without the patter of little feet.

Occasionally I'd get angry, not with my son, who was blameless, but just with the whole situation. "Why do I have to have a gay child?" I'd ask no one in particular. "Why do I have to deal with this? Why does he have to be gay?"

I don't know if you've experienced this, Mary, but one of the most unsettling feelings I had in those early weeks was the feeling that I could no longer trust my own perceptions. It was like my world had been turned upside down and things weren't what they seemed. If I could miss the fact that my own son was gay, what else was I not seeing clearly? I thought I had been a good parent, but had I? I thought he had a happy childhood, but did he? It was necessary to affirm those perceptions by asking for input from others, especially my son. His answer to both questions was, "Yes."

My shaken perceptions gave rise to a lot of doubt and misguided self-questioning concerning my role as a parent and where I might have gone wrong. At this point I mistakenly believed that I must have failed somewhere because I had a gay child.

One of the things that helped me was the advice I got from a lesbian friend who was also the advisor of the Student Gay, Lesbian, and Bisexual chapter in our community. When I expressed my anguish, my fears and concerns to her upon

hearing the news, she said quite simply: "Get educated." I took her advice to heart and read a lot of books. I joined our local Parents, Families, and Friends of Lesbians and Gays organization. I read their informative materials and talked with other parents. Slowly, the dark cloud lifted and I was able to see the sun.

I know you are probably feeling very alone now, Mary, and without a lot of support. I remember when my son came out, he asked us not to tell his grandparents because he was afraid the news might disappoint them. I want you to know, Mary, that you are not alone. There are thousands of parents each year who struggle with these issues and go on to enjoy wonderful relationships with their gay children. This is my hope for you.

$\mathcal{F}$riends and Family

Dona McGovern
St. Cloud, Florida

Dear Mom,

You were absolutely right! Just when I had given up men completely, the most perfect man walked into my life. He is blond and has blue eyes I could fall into forever and the really incredible part is, he listens. And I don't mean listens the way Dad does, from behind the newspaper or held captive in the car, which is about the only time he listens to anybody. Scott catches the nuance (my English professor is a stickler for vocabulary) and the concept of an idea before I've even finished explaining. And he has awesome muscles.

Don't panic. I haven't been giving it away or anointing his body with oil or anything. We were just sitting on a bench, talking the way we've done a million times, and it occurred to me that his body was as flawless as his intellect. And I'm writing because I was walking away from him, smiling like a Cheshire cat, and wanting to tell you how happy I was when I realized I haven't written you since I arrived at school because nothing has been happening. And now it has. Well, it hasn't really but I know it will and I'd like to bring him home on Christmas vacation. If it's okay?

Give Dad a hug for me and pave the way. Tell him I'm having a tough time with biology and economics so he'll have some gripe to occupy his time. Actually, the courses aren't as hard as I expected. He'll be a beaming lighthouse when semester grades come out!

My roommate needs the computer so I'm signing off. She's sweet, but so immature. I'd like to take her stuffed bear and suffocate her one night.

Just kidding. Call you this weekend.

Love, Angela

Dear Angela,

So wonderful to hear your voice and to receive your letter the same day. Seems like our money is well spent and of course I'm glad you haven't given up on men. Even if many appear to be born on another planet, including your father, they can be a wonderful complement to the feminine endeavor. And they've ruled the world so long it must be very hard for men of your father's generation to accept the changes women have brought to business. Only yesterday he was complaining about a female partner brought into the firm. I had to stifle a laugh when he was telling me how she refused to make a pot of coffee when he asked and he called her pigheaded.

Scott sounds special. A man that can calmly listen and not make hasty judgments has to be a jewel. I can't wait to meet him and promise to smooth the rough water in advance of your visit. Oops, you live here. Sometimes I wander into your room looking for the cat and it seems you have left forever. I won't be maudlin (add that one to your vocabulary) but only remind you to be very careful in the first flush of love. It may heat your cheeks but it can cool the sight of your goal. And I have the utmost faith in your ability to graduate with a useful degree without allowing your typical flightiness to interfere.

Everything here is fine.

Love, Mom

Dear Mom,

I don't want to cause you undue expense by using the phone. You always worry about money. Dad worries about everything, but mostly about me and you know I can take care of myself. Not enough people worry about the important things, like the way someone can enter your life and make it more valuable. Or the way material possessions seem stupid after a while. That's why I'm handwriting this and not calling.

There's no way to make you understand what I have to say and how crucial it is that you tell Daddy how much I love him before you tell him the rest. I love you, too, and know that your heart will recover from this "supposed" injury much sooner than his. Anyway, I neglected to tell you that Scott is the custodian in my dorm for the very reason that you would put more importance on his salary than his total commitment to our relationship. And you might slip in one of those heart-to-hearts you have with the "girls" at the club and it would come back to Daddy through the grapevine and make me look like I wasn't grateful or that I didn't care about you guys and that's not true. An axiom (you seem to think words are so important) for one person could be a catastrophe to another. That doesn't mean the world has ended.

School's not for me. The stress is unbelievable and everyone but Scott thunders around this place as if there's a four-alarm fire. I'm just going to take a semester off. Don't have a fit. I promise to learn a new word every day and pay back every penny when I get a job. Take care of Daddy. I can be reached at P.O. Box 77612. You know the rest.

Big kiss, Angela

Baby,

Take the semester off and enjoy yourself. I once took a year off from your mother for a little sojourn of my own. A brief respite I am not proud of, but which left me energized and more appreciative of what I had left behind. I've enclosed a check and a picture of your mother and me on the neighbors' boat. If your mother looks seasick, she was! It has nothing to do with your decision to drop out and take up residence with a janitor. We both feel that he has excellent taste.

Please call me at the office if there's anything you need. Mom might not respond in her usual candid manner. She's been ill ever since our deep sea excursion.

Keep in touch, Dad

Hello,

Life is placid (still have my thesaurus) and I'm still planning to show up for the holidays. I hope you put the lights up on the roof. Instead of Scott, I'm bringing this guy I work with, the head chef where I work, because things didn't work out with Scott and Teddy said he never spent Christmas in a house that put up decorations. He's really perceptive and when I told him about Mom's seasickness he recommended this really great cure the sailors used when he was in the navy. Don't take any cruises until I get home!

Hugs, Angela

Dear Angela,

Your father and I spent the afternoon taking down the Christmas lights outside and also the strands you hung all over your room and in the kitchen. We were so sorry you were unable to bring Teddy, but thought your friend Krystal was interesting, if a bit masculine. I have never met a woman welder and I must say she has a very unique sense of fashion.

I am still recuperating, but was able to rise the day after you left. Your father tells me you and Krystal are moving to Alaska to pursue careers in the art field. Pack appropriate attire. One thing I admire about the Eskimos is their proper diet of fish and caribou, completely without additives.

I'm doing a total renovation of the house. It seemed so conservative and stuffy after you left. Your father is furious about the money, but I know he'll be pleased with the Turkish effect. He has moved into your old room where I've added a few wall-hangings and camel hair stools. My room will have an ornate and heavily ostentatious bed. Perhaps instead of a computer and thesaurus I should have started you on picture books covered with tapestry and tassels. Your friend, Krystal, made a good point about making the bedroom a prurient place of worship. You must bring her back for another visit sometime.

Send her my love, Mom

The Daddy Bond

Suzanne W. Paynter
Richmond, Virginia

During the first several months of my son, Orry's life, I was his "one and only," his Queen. Sometimes I felt overwhelmed in my new role. "Why can't someone else breast-feed him? Put him to bed? Make him stop crying?" I asked in my sleep-deprived, frustrated state. Well, recently my throne was usurped. There is now another "one and only," and his name is "Da-da."

You'd think I'd be glad to relinquish my role, relieved to have someone else in Orry's life so I can have a short break now and then. But as I watch the two of them playing and giggling, hardly looking up to say "bye-bye" as I leave to have an afternoon to myself, I don't feel relieved. I feel somewhat nostalgic for the days when I was the center of his universe. After all, how often does a person get to be the center of anyone's universe?

Oh, he still calls for "Mama" now and then, when it's 5:00 A.M. and he wants someone to play with, or when his poopy diaper has overflowed and needs changing. But after a full day of feeding him his favorite foods, taking him to the parks with the best slides, and searching the house for his lost "Boo-boo" because only "Boo-boo" will do, who does he beg for, whose name babbles from his sweet lips 157 times a day? That's right, "Da-da."

I wonder when this tighter-than-glue Daddy bond began. I felt the first stirrings of a bond with my son the night I stared unbelievingly at the clear, blue line on the home pregnancy test. One minute I was just me, and the next I knew I held a tiny life inside. That magical night was only the beginning of a bond that has grown stronger with each passing day.

But I don't think the "Daddy bond" began that way. There was something about the way Da-da held his newborn son that said the Daddy bond was going to be a gradual one. Now don't get me wrong. I'm not comparing amounts of love here. My husband loved his son as much as I did from the moment he held him in his arms. But it looked awkward to me.

The other night I asked my husband when he thought his bond with our son began. "Be honest," I asked gently. He was quiet for a minute, then answered.

"In the beginning I felt a strong sense of protection. He seemed so small, so fragile. But he was just like a blob lying there. I mean, he didn't *do* anything. But then when he was about four, maybe five months old, he started moving around and sitting up. We could take baths together, and I could wrestle with him a little without feeling like he would break. I remember going into his room at night and watching him while he slept. I just wanted to hold him to be sure he was real. But I didn't want to wake him so I just watched him sleep. I felt such a deep sense of love. I guess that's when I really began to feel a strong bond with him."

So these days it is Da-da and Orry having bath time, Da-da and Orry getting dressed, Da-da and Orry going for a bike ride. And when it's time for Orry to go "night-night," I hug him and rock him for a few precious minutes before Da-da sneaks into the room. Then I'm forgotten as Orry lunges out of our cozy cocoon into the arms of his "one and only." And that's okay. Now that he's discovered Da-da and made him King he has twice the attention he had when only his Mama was his Queen.

The Power of Mom

Marion Franck
Davis, California

The call comes to my office at midday.

"This is Penny from your son's school."

Steve is in third grade and not a troublemaker. He must be sick. Even before the school secretary speaks again, my hand tightens on the receiver and my mind goes into overdrive. What appointments do I have this afternoon? Oh no, a meeting that has been planned for two months is supposed to begin at two and last until five. Who can babysit? Christie? Beth? Cameron? Will they mind watching a sick kid? Will I be able to reach them at this time of day? What time is it anyway? I'm thinking so hard I can't focus my eyes on my watch.

"Steve says he has something in his ear."

"Something in his ear?" This is unexpected. New. Not contagious! Maybe Steve can stay at school, since I won't be able to get a doctor's appointment right away, anyway. I can go to my meeting. Selfish relief floods through me like an illicit drug.

"Steve wants to talk to you."

"Mommy?" He's years away from an adult voice, but his chirp sounds husky and male, especially now when he breathes shallowly between each word.

"There's something in my ear, Mommy. I can feel it."

I answer with the calm intensity of the cowboy as he waits motionless on his horse, watching the Indians come over the rise, "Tell me about it, Steve. When did this happen? Did somebody put something in it?"

"No, Mommy."

"Does it hurt?"

"Not exactly. It's bugging me."

Another child might do this for attention. Steve himself might pull that at home.

But at school? In the office? Missing lunch? "Bugging him" must be serious.

"Okay, Steve. I'll come. I'll stop home first and get some stuff, then I'll come."

The job I leave to rush to him is a new one, and in it I feel powerful. I am a judicial affairs officer at the University of California, Davis, and I spend my workday confronting college students who have broken the rules. We meet, talk about the exam on which they cheated or the fire alarm they set off, and we discuss punishment. Often, my decisions control the students' immediate future. Most don't call their mommies. But I shake their hands before and after our meetings, and I can vouch for the fact that palms do sweat.

I affect college students, but in reality I control my son's fate far more than theirs. Steve's life, from the food he eats to the bed he lies in, from the hamster he loves, to the allowance he hoards: all is controlled by me. Yet, I don't think about that power, I just live it, day by day. Since I commute to work by bike, getting home means fifteen minutes of hard pedaling. Again I'm list-making in my head, not babysitter possibilities this time but, "What should I bring? How should I get the thing out of his ear?"

I drop my bike, race into my house and grab a tweezer and a flashlight. I hope that whatever Steve has in his ear is near the surface and I can pull it out. Or maybe I can float it out. I fly from the medicine cabinet to the kitchen cabinet but I can't find the ear drops. Frantically, I check the bathroom one more time. Well, the drops are for swimmer's ear anyway. I'll do without.

I am buzzed by a slight awareness that I'm hungry and missing lunch. I jump into the car and careen down the eight blocks and around the four corners between me and school. Steve is waiting in the office. His little face is intensely serious as he looks up at me; then he rises silently and sucks in enough breath to make him taller.

"I'm going to try to get it out, Steve. Shall we do it in the car? Would you like privacy?"

I see the answer in his quick move to the door and out into the parking lot. I open the slider of the van and he climbs in, throws himself across the bench seat and wails. I guess I won't be examining the ear right away. I open a window. He jerks up and closes it. Privacy and tears and Mommy, that's what he wants.

So I sit next to him and draw him onto my lap and hug him hard and he tells me he's scared and he asks, "Will we go to the doctor?" and "Can we get it out?" and I tell him, "Well, I haven't seen it yet. Do you want to let me look?" Damn these bifocals. I strip my glasses off, click on the flashlight and lean close to his ear.

"Let me see the other one, Steve. I need to know how it's supposed to look."

Docile, he turns over on the narrow brown seat and I point the flashlight at his other ear which doesn't have a white spot inside.

"There is something in there, Steve. The other one's not the same. You want me to try to get it out?"

How little I know about ear anatomy. I stretch the lobe, then the side, then I insert my tweezers (not deeply) and yank. I think I've grasped something but when I look at the tweezers I only see wax. I peer into the ear again and near the surface I observe the white, slight bulge of something that makes me think of a wrapped candy or a tiny piece of bark. What is that?

Steve is sitting up now, pulling on his ear and telling me that it feels different depending on which way he pulls.

"But it's not out, Mommy. Get it out."

I think about the fragility of an ear and infection and physicians and how hard it is to get an appointment and how much I want to go to my meeting. Self-interest and concern for my child intertwine so closely, like the strands of an umbilical cord, that I often can't decide what's what.

"Ok, Steve, one more try. Lie real still."

 *Defining Motherhood*

Abandoning the flashlight, I press my face close. I push the tweezers in just a little farther than last time, and Steve stiffens. I squeeze on something and yank. He moans and I wonder if I've snagged an ear part that's supposed to be there, something I shouldn't have touched. But I feel movement, so I pull gently and in a moment, the tweezer is out, its jaws holding something square and yellow-white. The object is small and firm between the tweezer points. I drop it into my hand and peer at it from another angle. It's not a tooth, but...oh, I see!

"Steve. It's out. Guess what it is? A kernel of corn. Can you believe that?" He raises his head and observes in wonder. I ask the obvious question, but he seems to have no idea how it got in there. Then his weather changes and he grabs me around the neck and starts to sob. The tears come in gales and his hard, long breaths beat like wind. I pull his little body onto my lap again and hug him close, surrounding the sobs with my arms. Hear my heart, little boy.

If there was ever a mom job—rush to help, perform the miracle, comfort the tears—this was it, rolled into the movie script of a hair-raising bike ride, equipment seized from home, transferred to the car, rushed to the school. Did ever a cowboy pull together a posse as fast as I? I've got my silver spurs and I protect the weak and powerless. I pulled out that varmint and saved my son.

I am woman, call me Mom.

Terrible Twos

Gwen Soffer
Swarthmore, Pennsylvania

All new mothers are warned about the "terrible twos." Well, I discovered on my own that the twos are far from terrible.

I am seeing my two-and-half-year-old daughter, Maddie, at perhaps the most positive stage of her life. Everyone emphasizes the "no" that comes from a two-year-old, but it is the "yes" that I cherish the most.

Everything is exciting and interesting to Maddie. She wants to know "why" and "how." "Show me, show me," she repeats with endless enthusiasm and curiosity. The world is something she wants to learn about and explore.

As far as the "nos" go, I value them as well. I want my daughter to be strong-minded, confident, and sure of what she does and doesn't want. I encourage her to make choices and not to listen blindly to authority. Of course, I grow impatient at times just like everyone else, but I always try to remember how important it is for her to discover herself and the power she holds within.

Mother's Return

Tammy Parr
Minneapolis, Minnesota

When I sit back and think of all the positive changes that have occurred in my life as a result of becoming a mother, I must first acknowledge my good judgment for choosing to accept responsibility for what many considered a "mistake" and for giving birth to my daughter.

Like a growing number of women, I was young, single, and quite selfish. I had a high school diploma, a job going nowhere, and spent most of my free time and money at the beach or bar. Not only was I not in a financial position to support a baby on my own, but I realize now that I wasn't emotionally prepared, either.

I was twenty-one at the time, and despite my uncertainty about my future plans, I was confident that I knew everything necessary to embark on this journey. I have since crossed the threshold that separates maturity and immaturity, at which point a person acknowledges the fact that she knew nothing at all and still probably doesn't. What I realize as a single white mother of a biracial daughter is that I will continue to face hurdles I had not bargained for, and that this journey is one that submerged me in two worlds I knew very little about: the world of motherhood and the African-American experience.

My daughter, Yaboday, Nigerian for "mother's return," added a dimension to my one-dimensional life. Although I didn't know it at the time, the dramatic change that occurred in my life when my daughter was born three-and-a-half years ago laid the foundation for many more changes to come.

I suddenly became interested in race and gender equality issues. As a parent, my biggest concern became protecting Yaboday from the evils of this world. The thought that one day she would face many of the same challenges that I faced as a woman, motivated me to take action. And by taking action, I simply mean I stopped being a passive observer and started searching for resources that would teach me so I could teach others. The fact that my daughter is biracial forced me to take a stand on issues of racism where, I'm not proud to say, I never had before. It is also because of her race that I willingly relinquished many of the privileges I was afforded simply because of my white skin, the most important being ignorance.

It is because of my daughter's need to have a mother that I've put limits on aspects of my lifestyle that are potentially destructive. It is because of her future that I now set goals for where I want to be five, ten, and fifteen years from now.

Finally, it is because of my elevated self-esteem (the result of everything above) that I am ambitious, motivated, and driven to be the best mother, friend, woman, and spirit that I can possibly be.

It is because I am a mother that I have discovered the insignificance of "things" and the importance of goodness, love, honesty, kindness, generosity, tenderness, loyalty, and understanding. My desire to be an example for Yaboday has forced me to look at my own habits and make the necessary changes because I know she will learn more from the way I live my life than from anything else. In doing so, I will have the joy of watching my gentle, witty girl develop into a strong, intelligent, loving, compassionate, and assertive black woman.

The Second Time Around

Nydia E. Rodaniche
San Antonio, Texas

"Yes, I'm pregnant again," is how I matter-of-factly respond to people who see me in maternity clothes. I guess what surprises friends and family about my second pregnancy is how close my pregnancies are. I do, after all, have a twenty-one-month-old, get-into-everything, test-mom-and-dad-to-the-outer-limits-of-parenthood, rambunctious toddler who exclaims, "Oh, oh," every time I back out of the driveway. And yes, by the time my son turns two years old, my second child will be born.

Does it bother me if people think that a career mom with an MBA degree is not taking her career seriously enough? Let's just say that I am not losing any sleep over it.

I was not trying to get pregnant so soon. I had planned on waiting at least until my son turned two before trying for my second child. When the test came back positive, I was shocked and surprised, to say the least. If a swarm of bees had flown into my mouth just then, I wouldn't have noticed. When I broke the news to my husband that we were expecting again, he smiled, hugged me, and muttered to himself something about hibernating next January. We had, once again, conceived in January!

When my next-door neighbor with three kids learned I was pregnant again, she could only exclaim how foolish I was and asked what had made me do it. I told her, "Boredom. We didn't have anything to do," and then laughed. More wise and consoling comments from other people followed. The most popular words of wisdom have been, "It's good to have them while you are young. Get it over with soon!"

I'm beyond that now. Feelings of excitement, elation, and joy fill me. I day-dream about my children playing in the backyard in harmony, and then pulling hair or toys from one another. I also look forward to watching my children become friends.

I am excited about this pregnancy even though I already know what it is like to wake up nauseated and feel like the last meal I had was the worst meal. I also know what it's like to put away my favorite blue jeans for more than the summer months, until they fit again, two summers later. I've done that before! I also know the excitement of feeling the baby move for the very first time. I know the pain of birth, the grunting, groaning, and grimacing that comes with every push. From my husband's perspective, delivering a baby might seem like passing a watermelon! I know that I won't look like the glamour gals from soap operas when they are in labor. But hey, if my husband videotapes this birth, I'll feel like a celebrity. I also know the joy of holding my son for the first time. But one thing I don't know is the joy of holding my second child. I haven't been there yet. I can only imagine the joy and pride of going through this a second time.

Maturity

Dona McGovern
St. Cloud, Florida

I let my son pluck the first gray hairs that erupted and threatened to pepper my middle-aged mane. Then I told him to stop when the silvery threads become as much a part of my demeanor as his childhood antics. I allowed him to light fireworks and sleep in the tree house all night long after he was embarrassed by the worn loafers I wore to parents' night. The piercing music and baggy pants will peel, like onion skin sunsets, and seasons slide off the horizon—in this rush for maturity.

My twenty-year-old son is on a ship in the China Sea and his fiancée's grandmother calls to tell me the engagement is off. I look at the engraved invitation, navy blue letters on white to match his uniform, tucked beside a fifteen-year-old family photograph and see his little boy face swimming in a sea of smiling sisters.

Instinct demands I protect him from the fallout the way I always did when a bully or teacher undermined his self-esteem. I see villains threatening to tip the precarious balance of his scales that have leveled with the passing years, and now promise a future. I am angry with the weight of this knowledge, the audacity of the grandmother to put me in the heart of this hurricane, and the speculation swirls and picks up speed. I exhale and rotate my head slowly in the circular movement I learned in my stress-management class to release the tension in my neck muscles.

His birth, 10:04 the morning after my water broke in the grocery store. His father too nervous to attend even after the Lamaze classes. A flash flood of concrete moments creeps up a chilly wall. Breathe deeply. Let it go. The fancies fade.

Minutes later, my ex-husband phones after receiving the same call and tells me the long-range outlook is probably for the best. There is a renewed warmth in knowing you share fear for your son and you both want to protect him. We decide we should both write him immediately (and calmly, my ex adds with that little laugh that slides reassuringly over the phone lines like a cool breeze) because secrets have the power to take on a nasty life of their own.

The letter I write is short and supportive and though I am loathe to give my grown child advice, I suggest he promptly contact his fiancée. Twenty-eight lines that take me two hours to write because all the images of his curly haired youth come flooding back in a maternal tide that keeps sweeping me away from my purpose. There is a mental picture of him drawn from tender memory, looking at me over the metal mouth of a harmonica with wide two-year-old eyes full of trust. It seems a lifetime since my child gazed at me with so much faith and I thank God for having given me this gift. All the foolish plans I had of being friends with my son faded in the harsh glare of his adolescence, only to come back full circle in his adulthood to a place where that dream was realized. Firm ground where I have his respect and his friendship, where it is no longer important what kind of mother I was, but only that I would always be his mother.

Of all the degrees and awards my son received, I am most heartened by his words. The letters, the phone calls, the stories that encourage the salt-and-pepper frosting I now wear with dignity.

Last year, in class, a sergeant requested that each Marine stand and identify himself by first name. My son stood and barked, "Abel, sir."

The sergeant replied, "What kind of name is that, corporal?"

"Mine, sir," Abel answered.

"Your parents must have been stoned out of their minds when they had you," the sergeant said.

"Sir, yes sir," Abel answered.

I grin thinking of the class breaking up in laughter as the sergeant tries to maintain order. Perfect words from a child who was ready, willing, and able from toddler steps to Marine gait.

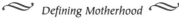 *Defining Motherhood*

55

The day after I send my letter, Abel calls to tell me the engagement is off. In the crazy time-zone shift I realize the news was passed simultaneously. Abel called his fiancée as her grandmother was talking to me.

As I age, more ironic twists and turns seem to assault me and coincidence seems less random and more a pattern that I've laid the groundwork for as fate tosses fast balls in my direction.

This pitch was a sidewinder and Abel was hitting with the aplomb of a pro. His acceptance that he wasn't ready for marriage demonstrates that he is mature beyond my wildest expectations. It was just another piece in the puzzle of motherhood that I neatly placed into the unfolding scene before taking a step back to look at the emerging picture.

The wide-angle view is breathtaking. There is a deep blue sky in the background that draws my eyes, the same way my son once tugged my long skirts and pulled me toward his latest discovery. In the center of the picture is the man himself, his stern façade broken by the tiniest twinge of a dimple forming in the thin cheeks that I covered with kisses when they were chubby. Surrounding the tall figure are images swelling and declining in a soft collage of moments and memories that identifies the viewer as his mother.

In the Beginning

Life with Newborn

April Burk
Archer, Florida

When my precious newborn was placed in my arms, I fell intensely in love and gushed, "She's the most beautiful baby ever born." In the following weeks, Sam and I gazed lovingly at our angel and knew life was filled with deeper meaning.

Yeah, right! Everything in the preceding paragraph is a lie. Well, not everything—I did give birth to Kayla. I want full credit for nineteen hours of labor. It would be nice to write a happily-ever-after story for when my daughter is older, but my conscience wouldn't let me sleep. Not that I've been winning any snooze-a-thons anyway.

As well-read as I was, nothing prepared me for the postpartum period. Articles can be vague with phrases like "big adjustment." I'm here to offer a behind-the-scenes look into the first month of my life with a newborn.

First week. When my crying baby loudly introduced herself, her hands were bluish and her head was covered with waxy vernix. I felt protective and soothing, but mostly I was relieved her birth was over.

The first days were deceptive. Kayla took to breast-feeding like a hummingbird to nectar. Full of energy, I actually told people this motherhood stuff was easy. Soon, however, stitches and hemorrhoids made me feel like I had a cactus clamped between my thighs. Books say babies sleep an average of sixteen hours a day, but Kayla got by on ten. "Sleep when the baby sleeps" is difficult advice to follow when your baby naps in thirty-minute increments.

Second week. On Monday, five o'clock came and went, and I realized that my job wasn't over, would never be over. I hadn't been prepared for a baby who cried every time I put her down. She reminded me of a leech. I felt tired, incompetent, trapped.

During one of Kayla's crying jags, I put her in the crib and gave myself a time out. I listened to her scream, did deep breathing, and felt like I was abandoning her. After five minutes, though, I was able to pick Kayla up and calm her. But I knew I needed to get out of the house.

When Sam got home from work, we walked out to the field. It was wonderful to watch the evening fall as Sam picked blackberries. I felt liberated. Kayla enjoyed the outing, too, blinking at the contrast of green treetops against a brooding blue sky.

That night, I dreamed Kayla started to crawl. Before I could call Sam in, Kayla was walking and talking. When I woke up, I didn't need Freud to tell me to enjoy holding my daughter while I still could.

Third week. Kayla went through her first growth spurt. As a breast-feeding mother, this meant a few days of sitting while the baby ate. Occasionally, Kayla would doze, and it was during one of those brief naps that I started to cry. I don't mean silent tears. I'm talking hands-over-the-face wailing. When Sam walked in the door with a co-worker who came to meet Kayla, I was able to moan, "I'm just so tired," before I attempted a joke to put our startled visitor at ease: "Welcome to our happy home."

One morning, as Kayla drifted off to sleep, I felt heart-stopping love for her. What relief! I had begun to worry something was terribly wrong with me. I always thought mothers felt intense love at first sight of their offspring. Mine has grown gradually, and in talking to others, I've learned I'm not alone.

Fourth week. There's nothing like sleep deprivation to alter one's values. One conviction that evaporated was the decision not to use a pacifier. It didn't take more than a few episodes of milk squirting up her nose for a frustrated Kayla to teach me that sometimes she just wanted to suck, not eat.

I read an article that claimed the first postpartum month is the biggest adjustment period ever in a woman's life. EVER. While dealing with an aching body, raging hormones, serious lack of sleep, and a changing relationship with her partner, she's undertaking a twenty-four-hour career in which a human being's physical and emotional health depends on her job performance. I guess I had every right to feel stressed.

Although I'm still exhausted at day's end, I'm intensely in love with my daughter and declare her the most beautiful baby ever born. Sam and I gaze at our angel and know life is filled with deeper meaning. Really.

$\mathcal{M}$y Journey

Andrea Shalal-Esa
Takoma Park, Maryland

March 1

Nursed Gibran five times for one hour each time. Changed his diaper eight times. Went for a short walk with him in front-pack. Showed Gibran the wind chimes on the deck: he smiled and almost giggled. Carried him in my arms for what felt like six hours but was probably closer to three. Folded two baskets of laundry, including two dozen diapers, while Gibran napped. Made dinner while singing silly made-up songs at the top of my lungs to keep him from crying because I wasn't holding him anymore.

I looked forward to my maternity leave. I'd been working hard since I was sixteen years old and figured I deserved a break. Fourteen years of working seemed like enough before taking a sort of sabbatical. Besides, I was looking forward to reading, writing, keeping a detailed journal of my baby's first year, freelancing some of those articles I never get to write for the wire service where I work, and I had the vague notion of taking a pottery class or perhaps starting work on my master's degree.

Three months after Gibran's birth, reality had set in. Not only was I not reading, writing, or freelancing anything, I had trouble keeping our house clean and even getting to the grocery store was an enormous challenge that involved careful planning so that Gibran wouldn't begin crying desperately to nurse halfway through the checkout line.

Toward the end of each day, usually during one of our prolonged nursing sessions, I found myself making lists of all I'd "accomplished" that particular day.

I made a conscious decision to drop out of work life for the first year of my son's life, to be there for him, to enjoy that special time with him and watch him grow. But instead of relishing each luxurious moment away from the daily grind, I felt guilty that I wasn't working on some "project."

Our society is incredibly output-oriented. We measure ourselves and others in terms of our achievements, accomplishments, and successes, like oh-so-many laminated certificates of merit hanging on the wall of a doctor's office. We define ourselves in terms of what we do, not who we are, and this becomes readily apparent when you stop "doing" things that are considered worthy of attention.

Another mother in my neighborhood who decided to stay home permanently after the birth of her second child told me, "I dread going to parties because inevitably someone is going to ask me, 'And what do you do, Susan?'" I was aware of the idiocy of this approach to life and often criticized it and rebelled against it, even before I became a mother. But I soon realized I was more caught up in it than I had thought. I realized my own ego, my self-esteem, depended in no small way on a successful listing each day of all I'd done, and compared with my previous accomplishments as a foreign correspondent and journalist, the lists I was making these days just didn't seem that impressive.

Perhaps, I'll say in my own defense, the contrast was exacerbated by all those media depictions of superwoman types who manage everything with ease and still have time to volunteer at the local soup kitchen. I've since concluded they must all be fictitious.

Of course, money was also an issue. I earn nearly twice what my husband, a professor at a small, liberal arts college, does, even though I only have a bachelor's degree and he holds a Ph.D. We needed both incomes to make all our house and utility payments and to eat and take an occasional vacation. We live well, not luxuriously, and now—facing at least six months of my leave without my income—we knew we'd have to cut corners everywhere. Mohamed, my husband, felt so pressured that he taught eight courses at three separate schools that year,

In the Beginning

just to help offset my lost income. I tried to freelance, but I didn't have the time initially, and soon found I also didn't have enough good contacts to generate a huge volume of writing work. But I knew we'd manage somehow. Besides, I didn't want to miss a single milestone in Gibran's development: that first smile, that glimpse of recognition, that "Oh, I know you!"

Two months later, he'd learned to smile whenever anything pleased him—the sun's reflection dancing on the living room wall, the birds singing, the blossoms of the lilac bush gracing our deck, the flitting squirrels outside. I was so glad I was there to revel in those moments even though I don't know if Gibran will have any recollection, conscious or subconscious, of those months.

May 5

I haven't written in months—I've been so busy. Gibran is beautiful, sweet, so gentle and loving. He is growing fast. He smiles a lot now, sticks his tongue out, bats at things, and studies everything intently. It is an absolute joy watching him grow. I am alternately in awe and miserable, because I'm not getting anything else done.

The months went by and we managed financially although my husband grew more and more exhausted. I also struggled with my own need to "produce," writing in my very sporadic journal one day: "I feel like I must be completely worthless if I am not accomplishing something, anything." Intellectually, I knew I was responding to years of conditioning by society, by my Mom (who, in her fifties, is only now learning to sit still and relax a little bit), the mostly unspoken expectations of my husband (although he did say once, "You have time all day, why can't you iron my pants?"), my own assessment of what others seemed capable of in similar situations, and so on. Yet, I seemingly could not stop measuring my worth in terms of such external values, even though deep down, I realized that spending day in and day out with my little baby, being there whenever he needed me, and creating learning situations out of the most mundane, everyday acts, was probably the biggest accomplishment of my life. I knew that, but I didn't feel like that.

 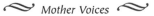

Instead, I felt inadequate on all fronts. I felt pressure to keep a perfect house, cook innovative new meals every day, exercise, and keep abreast of the latest world and baby news, be knowledgeable about all aspects of infant health and nutrition, all in addition to caring for our son.

There is a certain loss of time, of self, when you have a child. But it corresponds with an incredible gain, one that cannot be adequately expressed in words, for it touches every facet of your being. Suddenly, new worlds open to you. You are a mother, and you soon find yourself initiated into the secret society of people who give unsolicited advice, coo at strange babies, and make cogent observations about the size of their feet. Suddenly, people at the neighborhood farmers' market, spying you with bambino in tow, give tips on where to find organically grown rice cereal and the freshest carrots once baby is ready for solids. It's a warm world, pleasant, and one I never knew existed until I began venturing out with Gibran.

My life took on an even richer dimension with our family's entry into the neighborhood babysitting co-op. A wonderful group of fifteen families, most within walking distance. We meet once a month, and there are two different play groups that meet each week. We share advice, helpful tips, Band-Aids when our kids scrape their knees, kid-tested recipes, and many laughs. Our children all feel comfortable with one another and there's seldom a whimper when I leave Gibran with any of the families in the co-op. Being involved in the group also has given us a much richer sense of connection in our neighborhood. It's comforting to know that there are so many families I could call on in the event of an emergency. Many of the women in the co-op also decided to put their careers on the back burner while their children are small. In fact, I am one of the few women in the group who returned to work full-time. (I do the evening shift from 6:00 P.M. to 1:00 A.M., which allows me to spend all day with Gibran until Mohamed comes home and takes over the nightly duties of feeding, bathing, and putting him to bed.) Many others are freelancing from home, working temporary or part-time jobs, or running a home business.

In our hectic and fast-paced world, we aren't exactly conditioned to just enjoy life and take it as it comes. Ironically, that's what being a kid is, or should be, all about. Another way of looking at it is the difference between reaching your destination and going somewhere for the sake of the journey itself.

I struggle with myself daily, my insistence on doing far too many things at once, and my knowledge that these precious, glorious early days of our son's life will soon be over. It won't be long before he is filling his days with sports, music, school, and friends. I enjoy being a journalist, and my job is ideal because I have the best of both worlds: I spend each day with Gibran and every evening reaffirming my professional competence. But now, with a second child—and another long maternity leave—on the way, I think again about all I'd like to do while I'm not rushing off to work. I still want to get another degree, and I'd like to become more proficient at pottery. I did wind up taking a class, and Mohamed just gave me my very own wheel to work on at home. I've still got those book plans on hold, and all the while, I know that I won't do half the things I set out to do. I think about dropping out of the rat race and finding a way to work from home permanently, or reducing my work to part-time.

I only hope I'll be more able to enjoy those special moments with the new baby, and every day I try to take more time to be there for and with Gibran. Soon, not tomorrow, but perhaps the day after, he will no longer be interested in playing with me, or helping me weed the garden, or cuddling on the sofa for a luxurious afternoon nap. I want to cherish those moments now and forever. For this journey, after all, is one I'll never make again, and neither will he.

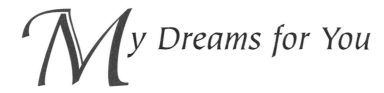

My Dreams for You

Mollie Yoneko Matteson
Livingston, Montana

What are my dreams for you?

I dream you will find your talents, and use them with confidence, purpose, and satisfaction; your creativity is the unique contribution you make during your tenure on Earth. I hope your fear, when you feel it, is the kind that is compact and distant, like a rock cairn on an alpine plateau, informing you where to go, what to avoid. Too often, fear can instead be a massive fog rolling in from the cold ocean, and either you are in it, blinded, or you see it hunched on the horizon and think your only choice is to run away. My fear has controlled me so much. I lived in that fog for years, and I think it would have seemed normal to me, except for the brief, occasional ray of sunshine that broke through the murk. Then I'd have hope, in myself.

When you can walk through the fog instead of abandoning yourself, you are exercising will. My Dad used to shake his head and say, "No willpower," when he'd see a fat person eating a hot fudge sundae, or an overly boisterous colleague at an office Christmas party helping himself to another cocktail. But will isn't about what people lack. It isn't about conquering your weaknesses, or punishing, coercing, or limiting yourself. It is about letting yourself be alive to the fullest extent possible. It is about intent and faith. Will is desire joined with determination.

May you be a "willful" child in the fullest sense of the word.

New Life Means Hope

Carolyn Bromley
Toronto, Ontario, Canada

We were told in prenatal classes to be prepared for the "baby blues" that we might experience a few days or weeks after birth. It was explained to us that we might cry uncontrollably for no apparent reason. Sure enough, the tears started in a powerful burst on the day I was scheduled to leave the hospital with my new baby daughter. However, for me it seemed there was a very identifiable reason for this outburst: this intensely personal experience suddenly felt so impersonal when someone out in the hall asked, "What did you have?"

"What did you have?" That's what it came down to. Boy or girl, and that all-important weight measurement, down to the ounce. To most people that is the end of it. They found out that I had a baby girl on January 13. She weighed eight pounds, seven ounces. Her name was Alison. That's it. It seemed so empty to me that this little miracle I grew and nurtured for nine months was reduced to that. To the majority of people she encounters, all she will ever be is a name. Somehow I expected the birth of my child to be special.

I suppose I wanted the world to stand still for a moment because the little life I nurtured was now in the world. Instead, Alison, just like every other baby, was issued her health card number and her "papers" to go. The people who had witnessed my belly grow large over the last nine months now had their curiosity satisfied. That was it. It seemed so...unspectacular.

In this highly emotional state, I announced to my husband that I wanted to take Alison up to the room in the same hospital where my father had died of cancer eight years before. Up I went, to the cancer ward on the thirteenth floor where I had not been for eight years, and walked down the hall with my two-day-old baby wrapped in a pink blanket, sleeping soundly. I peeked in some of the rooms and saw groups of sad relatives and friends gathered around their dying loved ones. In most rooms the patients lay alone, some with machines and tubes attached to them. Not surprisingly, I got many curious looks—a disheveled woman in a hospital gown carrying a brand new baby. When I got to the room where my father had died I stopped and looked in. I could only see someone's feet peeking from under the white sheet.

As I lifted little Alison Ann up to show her the room, her little arms flew up. This bold, lively response was, of course, a newborn's natural reflexes. She was unused to the freedom of being out of my womb. But, this lovely, life-filled gesture meant so much to me. Startled by the burst of vitality, I suddenly realized the real significance of this new little life. My little girl is the continuum of life—a chance for those closest to her to live on.

This has become so clear to me in the past four months. My husband, who worried excessively about the state of the economy and the future of the country, now comes home at night and revels in the growth of his little girl. He is continually delighted by her smiles. Instead of lying awake worrying about the future, he holds his little girl to his chest and quietly sings to her. My mother, a United Church minister, spends much of her time worrying about the lack of young people to fill her pews. For her, the sight of her granddaughter at the back of the church has given her renewed energy and hope. For the first time in a long time, she has hope for the future of her church.

My mother-in-law, who is always so careful to guard her feelings, giggles like a schoolgirl when she holds little Alison Ann, oblivious to the people around her. As for myself, I spend the majority of each special day at home with my daughter, savoring the feeling of the little baby in my arms.

For the first time in eight years, when I think of my father, the first image that comes to my mind is not a gaunt, dying man in a hospital bed. As I look at

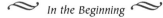

little Alison, I think of my father bursting with life and energy and love for his children.

As a teacher of twelve-year-olds, I am well aware of the challenges to come. But I also now understand that while the birth of Alison was a matter of casual interest for most people who know us, for those of us closest to her, Alison offers the promise of new life.

Outside Influences

Terri Webber
Miami, Florida

When I was pregnant with Claire (now eighteen months old), the advice I heard was generally kind. Most of it centered around how my life would change forever after the baby came. The comments were in good humor and generally congratulatory, except for an acquaintance who offered her condolences when she heard that I was having a girl, and another who described her thirty-six-hour labor in detail. Now that I am pregnant with my second child, the comments aren't quite as nice. Now I hear how exhausting two children will be, how awful it will be to have two kids in diapers, how jealous the older child will be, why did I want them so close in age, and so on.

During the first few months of motherhood, I found myself on the mailing lists of several popular parenting magazines full of negative articles. I know you have seen the headlines. "I love my kinds, but can't I lock them in a closet until they're ready for college?" With a newborn nursing every two hours, there was plenty of time to sit down and read, and at first I found these kind of articles amusing. However, after a while I realized that they were negatively influencing not only how I talked about my child, but maybe even how I felt.

Even the advertisements in these magazines influenced me. For instance, virtually every photograph of a breast-feeding mother (usually in formula advertisements) showed a baby at a bare breast. I figured this meant that I would have to buy a supply of button-up-the-front shirts and expose my breasts. Imagine how many other women have been influenced, perhaps to the point of rejecting breast-feeding completely, without even knowing why.

Many of these articles also stressed independence right from birth. I was warned that picking up my newborn every time she cried would spoil her and that if a baby didn't sleep through the night at three months she could quite possibly have a sleep "problem."

Why all this negativity? Perhaps because it is reassuring to know that no matter how bad your own problems are, somebody else's are worse. I admit I felt relieved after a friend shared with me a difficulty she was having with her own child, and I realized her child wasn't perfect either.

Since I recognize my own vulnerability to negative thinking, I read magazines where the routine put-down of children is not encouraged. I also make an effort to share my mothering difficulties without the "she's driving me crazy" attitude. I realize that change begins with me.

$\mathcal{J}$ust the Beginning

Marsha de Sylva Strickhouser
Clearwater, Florida

I didn't always want to be a mother. I didn't have ten dolls and want a big family. I wanted to be a writer. I wanted to be someone's best friend, and I wanted to have a lot of cats. But I didn't necessarily want to be a mom.

I fought it for at least ten years. During that time, motherhood was, to me, a banal existence of being tied down and shackled. It was baby food in your hair, dirty diapers, and not buying crystal. It was the end. But after seven years of marriage, several moves, and a hurricane, my husband and I both decided there must be something more. And that is when we decided to start our family.

Even though I wasn't sure I would be a good mother, once I was pregnant I knew I really wanted this baby. As my belly grew, I felt as if I had waited all my life for this experience.

The birth went "well." Chelsea Elizabeth took seven hours to be born. Everyone around me acted normal, but for me the whole world had changed. I didn't know who this little person was, but I loved her. I talked to her, sang to her until my voice was hoarse, held her, carried her, cradled her, and nursed her. I had a hard time keeping track of wet diapers and remembering on which breast I had last fed her. I had a hard time making it to the bathtub once a day. I cried at everything: cards from well-wishers, diaper commercials, my husband imitating the way Chelsea stretched before she went to bed. Breast-feeding was tough in the beginning. I cried. I ranted and raved. I cursed people for telling me breast-feeding was easy. I cursed people for telling me to try the bottle. But after two weeks, with the help of a lactation nurse, we finally got it and it became one of the best experiences of my life.

At three months, Chelsea started laughing and taking notice of her surroundings. It seemed like she blossomed. When friends with children came to visit we suddenly had so much in common. We talked about our children, what they were supposed to be doing, what to do about diaper rash or which stores had the best prices on baby items.

At the library, supermarket, or park, I found myself talking to women with whom I would never have spoken before, nor would they have talked to me. I felt a whole new respect for mothers. Sometimes when I was up at three in the morning feeding Chelsea, trying to keep my eyes open, trying not to slump off the chair, I would think about all of the other mothers in the world who were up nursing their babies. The strength of that bond kept me going.

I learned things about my own mother, too, about our relationship, about choices and decisions and sacrifices she had made. And I learned about my mother-in-law and sister-in-law and respected them in a whole new way for raising their children.

Becoming a mother was a burst of realization for me. Where had I been all of my life? Looking for the cheap stationery and power earrings?

Before I had Chelsea, I never thought for a moment that I would quit my job to stay home with her. It was out of the question. But that first day when I picked her up from day care I knew it was a mistake. So I quit. All I wanted to do was grow sunflowers and walk on the beach and read stories to Chelsea.

Since then, Chelsea has learned to crawl, and walk, and clap, turn pages in books, feed herself from a spoon, and peek around corners. I will cherish this year of being home with her, of talking to new mothers and sharing experiences, of bonding with my husband and Chelsea in our little love cocoon. And I now know, for me, motherhood isn't the end. It is the beginning.

 Am

Donna Tarr
Manhattan Beach, California

I am ditzy like a broken neon sign, brightly colored and partly incomprehensible. I am brave like a mother elephant protecting her young. I am sensitive like a canary overwhelmed by toxic fumes. To know me, however, is to learn my history. What I did, what I do, and what I will do.

I had a happy childhood and played a lot. I wanted to grow up so I could play bigger and better games. I grew up and became a bill-paying hedonist with medical and auto insurance who didn't disturb the neighbors. I indulged my senses. Sight: a movie every weekend and living as close as possible to a beautiful beach. Sound: crashing waves and ocean breezes. Taste: great food and alcohol and bottled water. Smell: sea foam and salt. I felt healthy and enjoyed my energy. I led a charmed life and I knew it.

Now I am a nursing stay-at-home mom, practicing another form of hedonism, depending on how you look at it. My day starts with a cry from my hungry little man and I go to his crib to retrieve him. His first hug of the day is like angels flying, or fairies singing—it is not of this Earth. Then I lug his thirty-five pounds, all boy and all baby, up the stairs and we collapse in bed. Daniel hungrily sucks with all his strength while I pretend I am a mother gorilla, elephant, or dog, depending on my mood. His head and body are warm and his muscles and flesh are firm, strong, and full of the energy necessary to do the thousands of movements they will do today. He tells me he wants to switch sides after draining one breast. What a lazy life just lying in bed. It seems like he'll never stop sucking so we can get up.

This new-mother period of my life has changed me in three major ways. I'm feeling more self-confident since the baby is still alive and he seems relatively happy. If I can stay home with a baby day after day, week after week, and month after month, I can do anything—except for right now when it feels like I can't get anything done. It is strange to feel empowered and overwhelmed at the same time.

I am no longer as self-conscious as I used to be. I've stopped caring about my clothes now that I've worn stains in public every day for two years. It can't be helped.

I appreciate time, quiet, kindness, and little things from deep in my soul. Going to the movies is now an event to get excited about and anticipate with butterflies in my stomach. A quiet cup of coffee while reading one section of the newspaper is a time to savor. A hot shower pounding on my tired shoulders is worth more than any gem in my jewelry box. Sleeping is now a pleasurable activity.

I look forward to being a selfish hedonist again someday. I'll be even better at it next time.

Melissa

J. Kristine Auble
Rochester, New York

She came into our lives and turned our world upside down. Instead of three-hour Sunday morning breakfasts, we have a crumpled comics section and graham cracker grins. Instead of leisurely candlelit dinners with soft music, we have hurried hamburgers, baby cereal, and a clown named Bo that squeaks. Instead of Cape Cod vacations listening to waves and seagulls, we have diaper bags and port-a-cribs and conversations with Raggedy Ann.

Instead of an extra hour in bed just holding each other, we have tiny hands holding our fingers and trying to put them into her mouth. Instead of weekends out on the town, laughing and dancing, we have little smiles that melt our hearts and feelings that bring tears to our eyes.

Instead of just the two of us loving each other, now there are three.

Abra's Song

Marianne Peel Forman
East Lansing, Michigan

These are the days of breast milk and burps that need coaxing. These are the days of walking my three-month-old through colic. Bouncing, swaying, rocking, humming old John Denver tunes, singing Simon and Garfunkel songs to the back of her head at 3:00 A.M. until she slumps over and rests her cheek in the palm of my hand.

These are the days when the dinner hour is raw nerves. My little one wants the familiarity of Mama, while my two-year-old wants to pick grapes in the garden, to thump a watermelon, to roll bare belly in her sandbox. I listen to my baby's screams when she is in my arms. I can convince myself quite easily that I am doing something to lessen her pain. But hearing her cry when someone else holds her is like hearing a faraway child gasp for air in the middle of a very deep lake. I have no rowboat to rescue her and someone has tied my hands and I cannot get to her.

These are the days when I find myself changing the endings of fairy tales. Goldilocks urges baby bear to crawl under the comforter with her just to cuddle, just to ease the hurt from the broken rocking chair downstairs. And the whole family invites her to stay with them. Not to scrub or clean or clutter herself with cinders and soot, but to be little bear's buddy and to share all future bowls of porridge and cream. Even the old woman who lived in a shoe feeds her children whatever she can find and hugs each child soundly and lovingly and tucks them into crowded beds.

These are days when I don't sing to my daughters as much as I thought I would.

My two-year-old wants to sing her own songs. She creates in her own words, her own melodies. I hum to them, sometimes, "Abra's Song," the gentle melody from East of Eden where grapes and lettuce all rich purple and green fill the Napa Valley. The rocking chair becomes my valley of green that I give to my daughters with my warm, soprano voice back and forth, over and over again, until they sleep gently, tenderly, in my midnight arms.

For the Sake
of Love

Priorities

Anne Mendheim
North Royalton, Ohio

Once Danielle was born, I knew that my priorities would have to change. I had not carelessly assumed the responsibility of parenting. Eric and I both considered it a joy and a blessing to be able to have a child and like our commitment in marriage, we both understood the importance of making our new addition a top priority. What I didn't anticipate was that in the first few months she was alive, Danielle would all but eliminate the remaining priorities in my life.

An infant can become all-consuming. And in my case that was an understatement. Danielle was a fussy baby and she needed so much. I was nursing, so, if for nothing else, she needed me for daily nourishment. Then she needed me to hold her constantly. She needed to be monitored during naps and stimulated during her awake time and frequent diaper changes in between.

Slowly but surely, other priorities disappeared from my life. I tried going back to work, but it just didn't seem right for me. If Danielle was truly a top priority, I needed to be home with her during her most significant hours. Having a career wasn't conducive to sharing precious moments with my most valuable asset. So I left behind the life of a college administrator and all the professional relationships, financial benefits, and personal perks that went along with it.

I barely found the time to talk to my husband, let alone to visit with friends or serve on community committees. In my limited hours of free time, I was too exhausted to continue my exercise regimen, pick up a good book, or enjoy the other hobbies that had once been part of my life.

As Danielle grew, she needed me in different ways: to take her places like from the couch to the coffee table during her cruising months; and to make snakes out of clay. I was an essential element in the game of hide-and-seek and I was the only one who knew how to read Winnie-the-Pooh.

I spent most of Danielle's first two years caring for her and cleaning my house, which still isn't clean. But I was very unhappy. There didn't seem to be anything to my life except diapers and Barney videos. I wrestled with going back to work but I knew that wasn't the answer. I didn't miss my job, I just missed the variety of experiences my life once had. The monotony of my days was making me resent my daughter. Finally, I realized that the problem was my prehistoric perception of what a stay-at-home mother was supposed to be.

So I started to search for the diversity I once knew. If my years as a professional gave me one valuable tool, it was the ability to network. I just needed to start networking in some different arenas. Like, for example, the library. I met some moms in the children's room at the library who told me about a play group in my area. I went a few times but it seemed big and impersonal, so I started one of my own.

Danielle and I enrolled in a creative-play class at the community center. I met the director of the center and offered to teach a writing class for children. It's only a few hours a week, but it gives me another channel for my creative abilities. I've also started to do some freelance writing, and I've volunteered to teach a Sunday school class at church.

Giving some of my time to these other opportunities has enriched my life and renewed my spirit so that I have more to give the ones I love.

I learned that a change in priorities should not limit my abilities. I am not proposing that I can do it all. I am responsible for drawing my own limits. I don't say yes to everything, but I am no longer afraid to add to my palette some things I have always wanted to do in addition to being a mom.

Lessons in Humility

Mary Rose Remington
Inver Grove Heights, Minnesota

Motherhood has provided me with some of the best lessons in humility. Pregnancy, itself, was lesson number one. Throwing up in front of my co-workers definitely knocked me off my pedestal. Getting used to my belly entering a room before me really took its toll on my ego. And how could I be anything but humble when my water broke while strolling down the frozen food aisle at the grocery store? "Clean up, aisle twelve!"

Lesson number two came during labor when I found out who truly had control over my body. Then came the breast-feeding. I remember nursing my youngest child every evening from 5 to 10 P.M. straight! I never did master the art of answering the door without a baby attached to my breast. My lessons in humility continued as the children grew older.

One day, my three-year-old son tried performing his first formal introduction while attending a New Year's Day neighborhood celebration. He made his way through the crowded basement filled mostly with men watching a football game. He proudly held onto the hand of his new friend and loudly, and proudly announced, "This is my Mommy and she has boobies!" As if that wasn't enough, the very next day he answered the phone while I was doing my business in the bathroom and said, "No, she's pooping," and proceeded to hang up. I have yet to find who that was who called.

During times like these I struggle to maintain what's left of my pride and dignity. But along with all this humility I have become more intimate with my real self, all pretenses gone. My children have put me in touch with what's real and important and what's not.

Going Back to School

Mary Junge
Eden Prairie, Minnesota

Come late August, my thoughts always turn to school. It seems I have been going back to school every September of my life—as a student, as a teacher of young children, and vicariously, as a mother. In preparation for starting school, my children and I peruse the school supply aisles of the local drug store, smelling new erasers and crayons and choosing the perfect paints. The smells take me back to my own childhood, to memories of tracing my once small hand; of standing on the front porch ready to start a new school year with freshly permed hair and a new book bag. When my children and I get back home, together we sharpen dozens of pencils, pack and re-pack the supplies. Our rituals are done with the air of anticipation and hope that only education evokes.

Before the school year begins, I hold fast to my fantasies of all that might be accomplished in the coming nine months—not only in my own teaching and studying, but also by my children. I know their strengths and weaknesses well. One is great at math but struggles with foreign languages. One is a creative thinker but needs to work on penmanship and self-discipline. One is so sensitive that I worry about him being bullied. They're definitely not perfect, nor am I.

Many of my own failings are glaringly apparent in abandoned summer goals and resolutions. I didn't exercise every day or organize the art cupboard. I didn't even attempt to make a dent in the fabric piled in my sewing area. And, I've read only five books from the growing "to read" stack. Still, I find that I can reflect on the summer with fondness—even the least pleasant times spent confined in the car going up north. I know that the details, memories such as one son singing to

 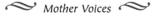

annoy his older brother (who then tightened the singer's seatbelt in retribution), will soon fade. We wind up the summer having knit ourselves tightly again during those long, full days together. The slowing of time was just what we needed.

In spite of the fact that I am a teacher myself, I send my own children back to school with a bit of reluctance. I believe that teachers' efforts to shape the character of their students far outweigh and outlast all of the facts they teach. Will my kids' teachers like them? I wonder. Of course I wish for them a good education, but behind that obvious, tangible wish is a shy, whisper of a wish that says, "Treat them well. They're my cherished children nurtured from babyhood. Now I entrust them to you for most of the day. I'm counting on you to guide them fairly and with great compassion."

Stitches in Time

Jody Rutledge
Arden Hills, Minnesota

Raggedy Ann lost her right arm this morning. Just one child-size year ago, Michelle would have shed sympathetic tears until the severed arm was securely sewn back in place. But now, just days past her eighth birthday, she keeps a stiffly immobile face as she examines the extent of the damage.

"My youngest daughter is growing up," I tell myself. Surely such a cool reaction is a sign of it. But even before I finish the thought, I know the truth. She has learned a survival skill—at eight years old my youngest daughter is hiding her emotions.

In my frantic Monday morning voice, I tell Michelle I do not have time to repair her doll. Michelle walks off to school without a smile, I drive off to work. In the solitude of the car, I can think clearly. In my hurry-up world of lost keys, lost time, and harsh words, I have lost track of what's truly important. We've forgotten how delicate and compelling the world is to an eight-year-old girl.

When I return home, Michelle is waiting for me on the front steps. She hugs me tightly and whispers, "I love you." It seems an act of forgiveness more than a declaration.

After dinner, Michelle carries Raggedy Ann to the sewing room and gently places her on the table to await repairs. Late at night, I pull needle and thread to secure the cloth doll's arm, all the time knowing that tomorrow is a new day.

Let's Eat Out

Lisa van Leeuwen
Rochester, New York

The waitress smiles at me as she offers me and my two lovely children a table. She has no idea of what is ahead. Already my girls begin to whine, and wait, there goes the water—the plastic cups go bouncing by and a lake begins to form around my shoes. I scold my darling daughter and the baby starts to cry. I am already beginning to lose my patience.

The baby throws his dinner roll and it spins across the floor. The waitress treads on it and it sticks to her shoe. The kids think it's hilarious. They laugh louder and louder and begin painting the table with their ice cream as it drips.

Oh, and we aren't done yet despite the fact that you can barely see the carpet through the food. At this point, my sympathy goes to the one who will clean up this mess after we leave. I tell myself I better have a glass of wine before I become unglued. My daughter gives me that sweet smile and says, "Mom, I didn't mean it!" I tell her to remove the straw that's hanging from her nostril and to stop drinking sugar. The waitresses are getting hostile, their dirty looks bolder.

By now, all eyes are on us. I try to hide my face and humiliation drives me to tears. I pray there is a way we can discreetly leave this place. I know we won't be welcomed back here for several years.

Getting Closer

Gwendolyn R. Nelson
Rochester, New York

They are getting closer…the muted thuds, thumps, and shuffles of twenty-eight small feet have left the gym floor and are now descending the stairway. A cacophony of voices, some shrill, some insistent, mixed with an occasional bellow or whine, floats down before the small army of children.

Going down the steps is a bigger deal for a four-year-old than for a grown-up. Those steps are nothing to me. I don't panic if the person ahead of me is a little faster or slower; it won't break my rhythm, my charm, my own special mantra that helps me navigate. I don't feel a rush of satisfaction as my hand slides down the clean, shiny railing in perfect timing with my body gliding next to it.

None of the children's voices is distinguishable yet. Does that mean I'm a bad mother, because I can't pick my child's cadence out of the crowd? Before motherhood enveloped me, I thought that any creature higher up on the food chain possessed the instinctive ability to identify the call of its own young in a crowd. As with so many other qualities that I had hoped motherhood would give me, that instinct eluded me.

Countless times on the playground or in the library, I go running with my protective hackles up, to rescue or comfort my child, and discover that he is playing happily, quietly, and another child has sounded the alarm.

The smell of the children wafts down the stairwell before they appear. Child sweat is so different from grown-up sweat. It doesn't have an offensive, foul, or musty odor, like locker rooms or dirty shoes. It has an innocent smell, like playing, running, jumping, trying to do something you're not quite big enough to do. It almost seems a shame to wash a child who's been all sweaty, except then there's a freshly scrubbed child smell to replace it.

The voice of the preschool teacher is distinguishable from the rest. A no-nonsense voice that is not raised or loud, but is somehow heard over all the other ambient noise in the stairwell. And—I marvel at this—the children do what she says. Any one child alone would declare mutiny and overrule a parent, charging full speed down the steps, but when they hear her special "I'm the teacher" voice, they all do just as she says.

The mothers, and one father, who looks as uncomfortable as I feel, are standing in the semi-darkness of the classroom waiting for the children to appear. If the children see us in the hallway, they will break rank and run to us before the teacher has told them it is okay, so we hide in the classroom to avoid tempting them.

Some of the mothers whisper together as they wait. About what, I'm not sure. I've tried standing next to them, but they don't whisper to me, and since I am eavesdropping, I don't feel that I can ask them to speak up or repeat things. Our children are the same age and go to the same school. Nominally I have some common ground with them, but I can't find it. I imagine them all doing educational and enriching family activities in every spare moment and I feel inadequate.

I feel like I should be enjoying this. I waited until I was older to have my perfect child, and now I'm taking time off to spend with him. I have a nagging feeling that situations like this should be fulfilling me in some deep, soul-satisfying way. It's like being a teenager again. I don't feel that I fit in with the crowd, but I can't think of any tangible reason why not.

I see them talking easily among themselves, and wonder why I don't seem to be able to think of anything to say to them. On the other hand, it is easier not to be involved. With adults, I can easily choose not to be involved, and no one challenges my decision. With a four-year-old, there is no choice. I am intensely involved. I am involved in every meal, every item of clothing, every bowel

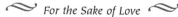

movement, every injury, every question, every game, every activity of every day, with precious stolen hours of my own few and far between.

They are getting closer, the little feet attached to fourteen sturdy, energetic little bodies, most of them about forty inches high and about forty pounds. It almost sounds like they should be uniform little squares, doesn't it? But each child has a personality so different and distinct there is no danger of confusing them.

I wait with a mixture of dread and anticipation for them to round the corner and line up in the hallway outside the classroom. I see the light of my life again, his hazel eyes anxiously scanning the crowd until he finds my familiar face. Then he forgets, as always, that he is supposed to wait for the teacher to sing the special "I see your mother, now you may go" song. She will remind him again, gently but firmly, and I will see him squirming, the look of desperation in his eyes, the near panic because he sees me and is still obliged to be across the room from me until he is dismissed.

They're getting closer. I will put a brave and welcoming smile on my face, and pretend I am strong and wise and know the best way to guide my son through the early days of his life. I will say goodbye to my private time, and my doubts and fears, my vague disappointment that I did not turn into the perfect, utopian Earth Mother when I gave birth. I will take his sweaty little hand into my own, and walk out into the sunshine, and into the rest of our day and the rest of our lives.

Acceptance

Maureen Webster
Stillwater, Minnesota

At three months old, Evan stopped napping during the day. He also woke up two, three, sometimes four times a night. That lasted for several months.

Gradually, he did begin to nap better, but only for an hour each day. He would still wake up at night wanting to have his foot rubbed or to be comforted back to sleep.

If he had four days of restful nights I began to think he was overcoming his "sleep problem," only to be awakened on the fifth (and sixth and so on...) with the same cries and requests. This pattern repeated itself for two years despite many efforts on my part to let him cry it out and teach himself to sleep, all with no lasting results. I was very tired when the thought came to me that maybe this was how Evan is, and will be, and maybe I was the one who needed to make the adjustment.

Maybe what it meant was his childish free spirit was so strong that it wasn't tamable. My childish free spirit was tamed long ago and this is the reason I feel so comfortable with the same things happening over and over, day after day. Evan became my reminder that a human being's life does not begin with order and control, it begins with chaos.

Evan's struggle to find his own sleep pattern brought out in me the parts with which I come into conflict. His struggle forced me to come face-to-face with the chaos that ruined my control in life and the control that squelched my imagination. When I let go of the control, my imagination came back. My understanding of what I am as a person and a parent became clear to me.

While reading the Little Princess to the boys, I was reminded of what an imagination can do for one's spirit. The character's imaginings keep her from dissolving into a depressive state when her father dies and she is forced to earn her keep. I've tried to do the same thing when I've had to rise in the morning after only a few hours of sleep or when the summer humidity and heat are unbearable and the kids have colds. I feel irritable and if I don't recognize the chaos and my inability to control it, the day can quickly fall apart.

I've learned that joy resides in the surprises, the serendipities, the synchronicities of every day. When there are no surprises left, then something dies inside of me. When I allow the chaos in my life and give it a place, but also remember to nurture myself, I don't feel so out of control.

It was a typical night in our household. I was attempting to comfort Evan, now a toddler who still didn't like to sleep. I was trying not to let frustration show in my voice and actions but it was nearly impossible.

"It's okay Evan, Mommy is here," I said flatly.

"Rub tummy Mama," cried Evan.

"Okay, I'll rub your tummy for a minute, then you close your eyes and go to sleep. It's late now," I said.

"Rub foot Mama, rub foot," Evan cried even harder.

I rubbed his foot and then his head, all the time hoping this would be enough. Then I walked out of the room after offering a few more words of comfort. His cries grew louder.

"Mama, Mama, rub tummy, Mama," cried Evan as I heard the clack of his pacifier hitting the wood floor.

I turned around and went back into his room to retrieve the pacifier, his comfort that he couldn't live without, the one piece of baby equipment that allowed us a few hours of sound sleep.

I slid behind his crib and reached for the pacifier. As I did, my head was next to Evan's, behind the crib bars. I looked toward the door to his room and saw an immense piece of wood that blocked my view. It was his door. Suddenly I was two years old lying in this crib and I saw how giant I must seem to my little boy.

I was bigger and more powerful and not very understanding tonight. All I wanted was for Evan to fall asleep. From what I could tell, all Evan wanted was a bit more comfort. By giving him comfort when he needed it, I, as the giant Mama, could show the depth of my compassion and patience. I would have to dip deeper into my well than I had before, but this night would be one I would remember as I began to truly see through my son's eyes.

I've tried to get Evan to change his sleep habits, but never had much success. He still sleeps some nights and wakes up on others. His security is in knowing I'll be there for him, no matter what. That's enough for me. I've tried to get him to become what I wanted him to be—an early-to-bed, easy-to-sleep, long sleeper. I don't see his not changing to accommodate me as an unwillingness on his part. Rather, the message is, "Mom, I have this need not to be orderly. I can't help it. Please help me like myself by accepting me as I am."

And I will.

*D*ay after Day

Tina Esposito
Los Angeles, California

I wake up at 7:00 A.M. to the sound of my eighteen-month-old son, Luca, playing with blocks in his crib. My husband sleeps. I tiptoe into my bathroom, hoping my son won't hear me. Each morning, I fantasize that Luca will continue to play so I can pee, slip back into bed, and get another fifteen minutes of sleep. Okay, I would be happy with five minutes.

I barely make it out of the bathroom and Luca is up calling me.

"Dadda." Yes, my son calls me Dadda, and his Daddy, Daadee. I get him up, changed, dressed, and downstairs for breakfast. My husband sleeps.

Luca eats like a teenager. One bowl of oatmeal, a piece of fresh fruit, juice, and milk. I chug down a cup of coffee. In between sips, I help him toss the strawberries toward his mouth, and away from the floor, the furniture, his ears, and his clothes.

I wash his hands and face and he gets up from the table. My husband makes an appearance.

David eats some breakfast. He has had time to shower, shave, and dress. As usual, he looks great. His entrance irritates me because his clean, lean body reminds me of what a wreck I am. Have I mentioned that my hair is sticking straight up, last night's sleep is still in my mouth, and I am in my nightgown? On a good morning, I have the good fortune of putting slippers on.

While David eats, Luca plays and I clean up the breakfast dishes. I have been blessed with a dishwasher, so I load it. I wipe off the gooey muck Luca left behind on the table. I sometimes wonder what it is in Luca's saliva that turns perfectly safe food into the cement-like compound that I need to scrub to get off the table.

It is now 8:00 A.M. David loads Luca into the car to go to day care. I should be on my way to work. Instead, I am on my way to the shower. Late again. I avoid the razor that would take the nub off my legs. The three minutes it would take to shave my legs can be better used for another cup of coffee. Besides, I am late for work.

Out of the shower, I realize it's garbage day. The diaper pail reeks—didn't I just take this out yesterday? I put on some makeup. All of my makeup has been relocated from a convenient drawer in the bathroom cabinet to a shelf high above my son's lipstick-loving hands. Returning to my bedroom, I see that my husband did not do the laundry as promised—again. David and I have a regular weekly conversation that goes something like this:

"Honey, don't worry about the laundry. I'll take care of it this week. You just take it easy."

To which I respond, "Thanks, that would be terrific."

The reality is that David has only done laundry five times since we moved in together five years ago.

I toss in a load and dash into Luca's room to straighten out his crib. I have convinced myself that the time I take to do this will save me some time tonight. I take out the trash, turn on the dishwasher, pour the coffee I never got to finish into a travel mug, and I'm out the door. (Remember those three minutes in the shower I saved to sit down and have an extra cup of coffee?)

It is 8:50 A.M. I drive to work. I am a community outreach and education professional. I attend endless meetings, make relatively important decisions, eat fast food lunches, and in rare moments of peace, dream of my son and miss the time we should have together.

I work through my lunch so I can leave twenty minutes early. I hope to use the time to grab a quick iced latté before returning home to get dinner ready. Somehow, I leave work and never make it to the café.

My husband picks up Luca at 5:30 P.M. and I get home by six. I heat up some dinner for Luca while unloading the dishwasher. I wash out the coffee pot from this morning and listen to my husband recount his day's activities. While David attends to Luca eating, I go upstairs and change out of my work clothes and toss the clothes I washed this morning into the dryer. We play with Luca for thirty minutes or so before I take him up to a bath. I wash my makeup off while Luca plays in the tub, then I wash and dry him.

Then we begin the battle of the diaper. Luca has discovered the joy of nakedness. He runs from room to room while I chase him, diaper in hand. As if I were not stressed enough, my husband makes an appearance to comment on how I should be better handling the situation. Being an intelligent person, my husband exits from my sight and I wrap the dreaded diaper around Luca's bottom. Luca goes to bed. It's 7:45 P.M.

I go downstairs and clean up Luca's dinner, start our dinner, and plan Luca's lunch for the next day. We eat and finally I feel somewhat normal. We talk, watch television, and read. Tonight, for a switch, David clears the table and loads the dishwasher. I mutter, "Thank you, husband, for helping."

I wonder why I am so grateful that he helped me with this small task. When did it become "my" responsibility to clear the table that he now "helps" with? When did the change take place? Didn't he cook and clean up after himself the many years he lived as a bachelor? He always had clean clothes on when we dated. How did his dirty clothes become my laundry to do? What magic ability do I possess that tells me that the dishes in the dishwasher are clean?

I realize if I continue this thinking I will drop into a gloomy depression, and frankly, I can't afford the time because it starts all over again tomorrow.

Healing My Wounds

Amanda Penel
Cammeray, New South Wales, Australia

Nobody told me that having children would catapult me into a journey of self-discovery. In the first two years of my children's lives I hardly knew them. I experienced constant panic attacks and was very depressed. I went from doctor to doctor with every illness known to mankind. Either my children had some weird disease or I did.

I felt very trapped, my head was in a constant obsession and my body in electrifying attacks. My family thought I had lost the plot and they had no idea how to help me. Finally, after two years of antidepressants and walking around like a zombie with no love or energy to give either of my two poor children or husband, I plunged into therapy.

It's been a long and worthwhile road of learning to get in touch with the many emotions I suppressed so well for so many years. Every day my son and daughter teach me something new about myself. I am finally learning to see them as they are. And more and more I am truly able to be there for them.

It's amazing how much my children mirror my emotional state. When they are needy, I get needy. I find I have to meet my needs first so I can meet theirs.

I am proud that my children can now express how they feel since I was never able to do that as a child. I really believe that healing my own wounds is the best gift I can give my children.

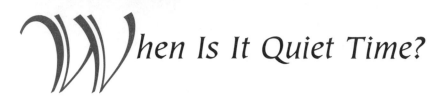

When Is It Quiet Time?

Sue Poli
Clementon, New Jersey

My legs are tired. My feet ache and only two chores are crossed off my list. When is it quiet time? Will the baby wake before I have had time to recharge batteries? Will I get that quality time with the kids that working mothers rave about? I've wiped and washed, disciplined and lost my temper, and taught and nursed, and nursed, and nursed. For me, parenting is an aerobic exercise, an emotional catharsis, an exhausting pleasure. My feet hurt…when is it quiet time?

If Only...

Gloria Watson
Bloomington, Minnesota

Until thirty minutes ago, I thought this had been a good day with the boys. Tonight, all I wanted was to read. One of my sons stayed up past his nine o'clock bedtime. We played checkers till he cheated. Then I said, "It's time to go to bed."

"I'm cold," he said. I gave him more covers. We talked about the "best thing that happened today." We always do. I do all the right things. I'm a Supermom, you know.

Then, "Mom?" he yells from his room.

"What's wrong?"

"I'm scared someone's creeping down the hall."

"But, I'm here. I would see them. Go to sleep, you're not scared."

"I want my Daddy! I want my Daddy! I want my Daddy!"

I want to read! I want to read! I want to read! SILENCE.

"Mommie! Mommie! Mommie!" SILENCE.

Have your way. You win because you are scared. I lose because I am the mother—the mother you need when she needs to read. A needed mother is more important than a well-read one.

One of Those Days—Again

Ann Cheryl Watkins
Philadelphia, Pennsylvania

D.J. has a river of mucus running from his nose, and he keeps contorting his face like a toothless old man so he can catch the stream with his bottom lip. Dee Dee denies knowing where her brother's toy airplane is despite the string dangling between her legs. Ronnie pops in and out of the room every few minutes to mournfully ask how much I will miss him when he leaves to spend the night with a friend, but when his ride comes, he runs out of the door without saying goodbye. My husband can't find his socks, his shirt, his tie...

If I hear one more whine for me to break up a squabble, look for a clean pair of shorts, retrieve a toy from under the sofa, or answer the same question for the seventh time, I'm going to run out into the street screaming, and I'm not coming back for the rest of the day.

$\mathcal{A}$ Mother's Right

Connie McGann
North Wales, Pennsylvania

I believe that as a mother, I have earned the right to be insane.

I have developed a "split personality" that emerges only when I'm on the phone. Strange facial contortions, grunts, and sign language indicate a personality unknown. My memory seems to be going and I fear Alzheimer's may be coming on. Some days I have to ask my children what their names are.

You've heard of false pregnancies? I'm beginning to think it is true. It happens when people constantly ask, "So, when are you due?"

Oh, and I hear voices…sometimes even in Sensurround, and I find myself yelling to no one, "Turn it down. I said turn it down!"

Alas, I keep asking my husband to let me rest in a "peaceful facility."

God bless us mothers!

Carrying On

Patty Super
Stamford, Connecticut

My husband phones me from his office in the middle of the day and informs me that his boss has asked him to attend a week-long seminar in Phoenix at the end of the month. My stomach muscles tighten. "You mean that you're going to be staying at a posh hotel eating at fine restaurants with colleagues while I'm alone at home with two small children?" He says he'll discuss it further when he gets home. I put down the receiver feeling angry, disconnected, and abandoned by the world of grown-ups.

While my husband sits in a lecture on fascinating new technologies, I'll be trying to figure out how to vacuum Cheerios from between unremovable sofa cushions. What's more, I may have to juggle my own work schedule—get up an hour earlier, skip the gym on Wednesday, and pick the children up from school and day care to accommodate his absence. Plus, I'll have added responsibility around the house. There will be no one there to relieve me—to take over when I need to run errands and get an hour break from the chatter of small voices. The situation feels unfair and dismal. What's more, he's a total chicken for telling me over the phone.

My husband travels for business a lot. Raising children in his absence is difficult. It can be lonely, emergencies sometimes arise and it is physically demanding. But I have a few basic strategies to make it easier on me and on the children.

I ask my husband to pack and prepare for the trip two days before departure. How the departure is managed is important. Last-minute running around makes everyone anxious. Doing something special as a family the night before he leaves sets the tone for the trip.

If a child's birthday will occur during my spouse's absence, I plan a party before he leaves. The child is happy his father was there to share the festivities. If a holiday falls while he's absent, we go ahead with the day and schedule a second holiday when he returns.

We arrange a mutually convenient time for both of us to check in by phone. I cannot be expected to wait by the phone and he need not be frustrated by failing to reach me after repeated phone calls. We avoid phone conversations at dinnertime or right before bed. Everyone runs a high risk of cranky behavior at that time.

I try to get help. If relatives or friends can take my children for the weekend, we plan to do that or spend the weekend at Grandma's house. This is no time to be stoic. I arrange play dates or sleepovers for my children. If there is one fewer child in the house, it helps.

I get my spouse involved in preparing for his absence. He goes shopping with me the week before he leaves—making sure I have plenty of easily prepared meals in the freezer and paper plates in the cupboard. The children and I can eat whenever and as informally as I like.

I have my spouse take care of any household problems before he leaves. If the sink is running slowly, I have the plumber come instead of waiting until my spouse is out-of-town and I have two small children crying for dinner. I encourage my spouse to anticipate problems. I resent his absence less if he takes that initiative.

Because some problems cannot be anticipated, I have a list of repair people— a car mechanic, handyman, etc. who can come to my assistance. And absolutely, I have access to the bank accounts. With my spouse traveling regularly, I must have the authority to make financial decisions independently.

I plan a date with my husband two to three days after he returns. It is usually too hard on the children for us to go out the day he gets back. The children will

For the Sake of Love

be very excited to see him and disappointed if he leaves again, even for the evening. I do not expect to feel connected to my spouse the minute he returns. It's normal to feel somewhat "out of sync." In fact, it can be nice—the first few days after he returns can almost feel like a honeymoon.

I try not to overwhelm my spouse with every household disaster that occurred while he was out of town the minute he walks in the door. He won't be able to listen and I'll feel frustrated.

I expect my children's behavior to be affected by the trip. The first few days after my husband's departure, the children are angry. They will act out their anger on the adult who is present—me. They tend to idealize my spouse during his absence. Then, when he returns, it is difficult for the children to accept two authority figures in the house.

The most important aspect of surviving spousal travel for me is to accept the situation calmly, compassionately, and rationally. I try to keep in mind that my spouse's absence was probably not his idea. His employer does not usually give him a choice about these matters. It's part of the job and the purpose of any job is for a person to help support his family. My husband may feel an overwhelming sense of regret during his trip, regretting that he is missing some part of his family's life—that he is left out.

As for my own regrets as a mother, it's natural to feel trapped when my spouse is traveling and I am expected to shoulder the full burden of caretaking duties. I try to nurture myself as much as possible both during my husband's absence and after his return.

ightmares

Tyra Novic Wahman
Shoreview, Minnesota

My mother claimed to have loved me too much. How else could she explain the nightmare she had in which she had to sacrifice me?

In her dream, my mother carries her naked, squirming daughter to a cold, stone altar. The surroundings are a typical fire-and-brimstone nightmare. She pleads, sobbing, with the unknown force to be spared this incredible ordeal, but receives no reprieve. Slowly, with hands that threaten to lose control, she picks up the icy knife provided and obeys. Her daughter's blood covers her hands, but she can no longer see. Her mind torments her only so far. She is spared the sight of her deed.

This nightmare, which my mother dreamt only once, frightened her for years. It confused her. Why would she have to kill someone she loved so much?

I was a young mother when I found out about the dream—too young to have begun my own nightmares, yet experienced enough to believe that the dream echoed the overwhelming demands of motherhood.

My mother wasn't comfortable with her parenting role. As a young mother, feeling constantly worried about the safety and comfort of her children, she sometimes wanted to run away and relieve herself of this burden. She used to tell us that she wanted to live alone, in a cabin far away. Somehow, we were supposed to be sophisticated enough to know that she was only feeling suffocated. When I rebelled as a teenager, she took my words and actions to be a personal affront, not seeing instead their natural, even healthy characteristics.

Assuming my marriage would be the lifeless, loveless lack of communication hers had been, my mother threatened not to come to my wedding. When I became

pregnant, rather than share the pains and beauties of motherhood, my mother instead informed me that she wasn't ready to be a grandmother.

Eventually, the pain and anger grew between us to the point that we could only write our disagreements to each other, in finger-pointing, hateful letters.

Then, the nightmare came true. In a letter that read like a stab to my chest, my mother told me that I had to learn to accept her as she was, even though she was angry and hateful to my family. If I couldn't accept her, she would walk away forever. Because of the anguish she had already caused, I chose to let her dream come true.

Long before this, my dreams had begun. My nightmares are of wells, deep holes, and bizarre caves into which my children slip. Usually I am with them. We are crossing the street or playing in the yard when suddenly one of them disappears. Immediately, I am sickened with the knowledge that I cannot reach them. One moment, life with Mother is safe and fun, the next instant fear grabs their chests and they don't understand. We reach for each other, and the look of shock on their faces haunts me. Why can't I exert my strength to rescue them? Because the dreams symbolize our future. I am reaching for my children in a world in which the natural progression of things commits them to slipping away. The dark holes they fall into are the unknowns in their futures: college campuses, new apartments, homes in other cities.

And the future is already here. When I send my children to camp for a week, or a friend's cabin for a weekend, I ignore, like all parents must, the nagging list of dangers they might face. Car accidents, drownings, stranger assault, sexual abuse; the list is endless and every parent keeps one. Reality is, however, that in order to keep them safe from these dangers I would have to take friends, freedom, independence, confidence and most of their joy away. In fairness to their childhood, I can't do it. So I bury my list instead, deep in my mind where it surfaces at night when my children's translucent eyelids flutter in sleep.

I am not immune to feelings of suffocation. I grow tired of my children's endless questions and requests to watch them dance or hear a joke. I would like to have an uninterrupted conversation with my husband, or a chance to watch a movie or read a book in silence. My children do take these things away from me and I don't like it, but sacrifice is a natural part of parenting. I have no intention of running from it.

My dreams convince me of my love for my children. My mother's dream convinced her of the need to leave hers. I am sorry that, for now, we cannot ease each other's sleep.

A Lesson from My First

Cory Gideon Gunderson
Lakeville, Minnesota

Resorting to prayer in times of need is a natural by-product of my parochial school upbringing. As I lay in bed, painfully aware that the life of my first child was in jeopardy, I silently rattled off the familiar: "Our Father, who art in heaven, hallowed be thy name. Thy kingdom come…" Although my thoughts in the last hours had been less clear than the pain that racked my body, I stopped my prayer abruptly and consciously in anticipation of the next line. Could I really mean "thy will be done," when nothing seemed as important to me as keeping this child of ours alive?

We had waited so long to conceive; this child was the answer to our prayers. From the first moment that I knew I was pregnant, life and all the answers to it filled me with delightful anticipation. In this situation, even acknowledging the words "thy will be done" seemed traitorous to the life that welled within me. I did not initiate the prayer to submit to a will higher than my own; I prayed as a plea to save the child who relied on me to protect his fragile life. Protecting my child was foremost.

I do not know what finally transformed me from willful protector to vulnerable servant. What I do know is that this time when I said "thy will be done" I understood the full weight of those words.

Our baby did die.

For a long time, I was as empty as I had ever been. Accepting the loss took time, and with time came perspective. In hindsight, I realize that my miscarriage was a turning point in my life. That loss was a critical wake-up call; it reminded me that life—and death—was not entirely within my control.

 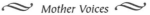

Seven years later, I am now the parent of two answered prayers, Katy and Luke. They continue to sound that critical wake-up call to me. On a daily basis, they remind me that I am not in complete control of my life—or theirs. I have learned that, besides the grander things in life that I have no control over, I must let go of the smaller things, too. I cannot determine what and when they eat; I cannot determine when they will be potty-trained; it is not up to me to determine what they will wear or who they will choose as friends.

This knowledge doesn't frighten me as much as it would have prior to my miscarriage—in the days when I prided myself on being organized, on being in complete control of my life. Mixed in with the pain of this life lesson, there is comfort in recognizing that I, alone, am not responsible for my life or the precious lives of others.

I continue to work at letting go. It is a lesson I learned from my first child.

$\mathcal{A}$ Secret Place

Mary L. Miller
Edina, Minnesota

Redbook magazine once published a dialogue between poet Robert Graves and actress Gina Lollobrigida. Mr. Graves asked her if she had a secret garden, "an imaginary place, a sort of living heaven of her own, in her mind, where she could go to be alone."

Somewhere between the peanut butter sandwiches and the piles of diapers, the PTA meetings and the piano lessons, the skinned knees and the tonsillectomies, the white shirts and the boss for dinner, the temperamental typewriter and the misplaced car keys, every loving mother needs to keep a secret place, a place of her own to store her most precious memories so that they may be taken out and looked at whenever and wherever the need arises. My secret place is where I wander in my mind's eye, and where no one can intrude.

Lest I be thought to advocate escapism, let me quickly dispel such an idea. A secret place is not an escape from the very real and very immediate problems and difficulties of mothering, but rather a place of solitude where one can gain a new perspective and a bit of calm in order to more effectively cope with those difficulties. I have often heard my friends say, "Oh, if I could only get away from all this for just a little while I think I could pull myself together and do a better job!" My secret place lets me get away for that precious "little while" without hiring a baby-sitter, spending any money, or even changing my clothes. Yet, when I return I can usually see things in a better light and there is a smile where before there was a frown.

I had a secret place even as a child. I should say especially as a child. It was my mother's that had been given to her by her mother; and it was a very real place in the beginning. I was able to wander through time and the lovely places of both my mother and my grandmother. Of course, now it really belongs to me and I will try to pass it on to my children little by little so that someday they may in turn pass it on to their children. I am sure it will be quite different by the time my great-grandchildren visit there; but I have no doubt that its effect will be the same.

Every child at one time or another says to her mother, "Tell me about when you were little." That was how I came to know about my grandmother's garden. It was full of wild flowers—columbine, bloodroot, hepatica, dog tooth violets, solomon's seal, trillium, pussy toes, and anemone. The garden was small, but there was a little stone path through it put down by my grandfather or the gardener at my grandmother's instruction. It was right outside the back door of their big, white house. To get to the garden you had to pass under an arched lattice covered with wisteria. I left my worries under the lattice, wandered in the shadowy, quiet garden for a while and then returned to the archway with renewed patience, bolstered courage, and perhaps a few insights into seemingly insurmountable problems. My grandmother was a rather round, comfortable person and I can so clearly see her walking slowly up the rock path gathering a bit of patience here and a smile there.

Now that I am grown, I have added another secret garden from my own childhood. When I was seven or eight we had a small back yard; and it possessed an enormous oak tree that faithfully dropped multitudes of acorns each year. There are so many things a child can do with acorns besides filling up pockets or saving them in boxes. I did that, too, but there were also acorn babies and charming ladies with handkerchief dresses. Besides harvesting acorns, we raised rabbits in that back yard to teach me the "value of money" and so that I might gain "business experience." The doe's name was Nibble and she had a hutch behind the garage. She provided me with six bunnies all named Jam because their muzzles looked like they had been into the jam pot. I believe my father bought the rabbits. My business records showed a profit of approximately $2.

That was a happy summer over and above the acorns and the rabbits. Without trying I can conjure up that house, my dog who played hide-and-seek with me, the back bedroom with the big, old upright piano and the spindle bed, the double-terraced front lawn I ran down barefoot every spring almost before the last spot of snow had disappeared, the bramble bushes my father mumbled something unprintable about under his breath every time they had to be trimmed, and my very best friend, Janny, who lived just up the street. I visit that house and yard often in my imagination. It is a pleasant, warm memory perhaps because I was young and happy and untroubled by adult concerns. It is easy for me to shake off my worries there, and to re-energize my immediate situation with some of that childlike enthusiasm and love of life I felt back then.

Of course, there are many memories I treasure from my marriage and from our son growing up over the years, but the wild flower garden and oak tree yard are whole and complete pictures that are old friends.

My husband has shared my secret place. During labor with our first son he held my hand and we talked of beautiful things. Perhaps it was simply a matter of concentration and quite a bit of luck, but I like to give the flower garden credit for making that time a happy one with very little discomfort. With the birth and almost immediate death of our second son, I found there was consolation and peace in my quiet memories. I could then face and cope with my grief and sadness.

It is not only the big problems I take to the garden. More often, it is the little ones. The harsh words and headaches can be dispersed and my small world set right again. I think my family, and even the dog, profit from my short escapes to that lovely, quiet place where all is at peace—the place where I restore my spirit. I know I am enriched and brightened by those treasured moments.

Letting Go

A Mother for Life

Alice Vance Collins
Bemidji, Minnesota

Parenthood is a lifelong commitment. Young people don't always comprehend that. I remember talking with a distraught young teenager who was attempting to deal with an unplanned pregnancy. She worried that she would be completely tied down for a couple of years! What a dreamer! No matter how old we or our children get, most of us find that there is a sense of concern and responsibility that never ends.

I vowed to stop worrying about my adult children one snowy January night, twelve years ago. I was awakened at 2:00 A.M. by the howling winds of a blizzard and bemoaned the fact that I had failed to suggest to my son, who was working late in town, that he come to our house to sleep. To get to his home he would have to travel a dangerous stretch of country road that was very susceptible to drifting. Restless and unable to fall back to sleep, I stumbled out to the kitchen to get an aspirin and discovered him asleep on our couch. There, I told myself, he doesn't need a worrywart mother anymore.

Recently though, he has had serious health problems that were life-threatening and, but for the timely efforts of medical rescue workers, he might well have died. It has been a time of worry for the whole family. I was staying with him in a hotel near the hospital where he'd had a major surgical procedure just a few days before. He wanted to take a walk for some exercise, but we were expecting a call to confirm his next appointment. He didn't want to wait and I sensed that he needed to feel he was regaining some independence. But he was gone so long! Several times, I left the room door open in case the phone rang while I hurried to a hall

window, pushed aside the curtain, and craned my neck, trying to see down the block and around the corner. I seriously considered abandoning my telephone vigil and rushing out to make sure he was on his feet when, at last, I heard him on the steps. He was back safely, having wisely taken time to rest on a bench along the way. My tense shoulders relaxed; I let out a sigh of relief and tried not to show how worried I'd been.

My thoughts went back to his very first day of kindergarten. He was supposed to walk the six blocks to school with an older neighbor boy, but his mentor ran off and left him behind. I saw what had happened and suggested that I'd walk with him, but he insisted he would be fine. He knew just where to go. After all, he was a nursery school graduate. Not wanting to admit that I didn't share his confidence, I watched and waited until he was out of sight around the corner and jumped in the car to follow at a discreet distance as he ambled along, arms swinging. He arrived at school on time, walked confidently to the right door and entered with his head held high. I went home and wrote a little poem about the experience which ended, "Then I drove home, mother of a five-year-old man." I guess I was a dreamer, too, in those days, but now I know I'll always worry about him.

Is Silence Golden?

Dolores C. McNabb
Byrn Mawr, Pennsylvania

The house is quiet. I know it will only be this way for a few minutes, but unmistakably, the house is quiet. I have just returned from a visit to my sister's house. Her children are grown. Her house is immaculate. When she needs to find something as simple as a piece of paper and a pencil, she knows where it is, and that it will be there when she looks for it.

I look around my home as I wait. Where my good stationery and pen used to be, there are now toy cars and crayons. Stuffed animals and toys are everywhere, and an accurate description of our existence would be somewhere between chaos and Munchkinland just as Dorothy's house fell on it. Yet, as I am looking around, there is something missing: all that crazy noise that brings the house to life.

When we first brought our new baby home, we found out very quickly that our lives would never be the same. The spontaneity of romance and Sunday morning loungings were exchanged for diapers, 2:00 A.M. feedings, and frequent visits to the family physician. Yet, it passed so quickly I sometimes wish I had been able to enjoy it more. I often wondered, "Will this ever end? Will there ever be a time again when I have at least one moment to myself?"

And then, somehow, I blinked and that baby was a little child struggling to take her first steps. Soon after that, I began that wonderful time of trying to rid the house of diapers—another monumental feat that I feared would never be accomplished.

Of course, during all of this time there actually were some silent moments. There was that time just between lying down at night and actually being able to

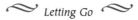

fall asleep. That time when I replayed the day's events—the good experiences sometimes completely overshadowed the unpleasant. If only we could reflect and use our experiences as learning tools rather than burdens to weigh us down.

Of course, along the way, there are many curve balls, like broken arms, stitches, school problems, and so forth. At the time, everything is a bit overwhelming, especially since my kids didn't come equipped with manuals. Yet, we got through it all, only to look back and realize that it wasn't so bad.

I am beginning to realize that everything is relative to what point in life you have reached. I was in church one Sunday, and a small child was carrying on, as church is inclined to make a child do. As her mother was taking the girl out, the women behind me whispered, "I sure am glad those days are over." At that moment, I was trying to keep my own five-year-old from squirming by rubbing his back. He thinks that church was invented to punish little children. Then, after the service was over, I was surprised by the woman in the row behind me who spoke to me with tears in her eyes: "I was watching you during Mass. You do the same thing to keep your son quiet as I did. There he is now. He's the altar boy up there. He's thirteen." I will try to remember this woman's nostalgia when the Power Rangers are turned up so loud that I feel like my son is actually entertaining them in my family room, and my daughter is arguing with me because I want her to finish her homework before we make yet another trek in the car to a ballet lesson, and I am trying to fit dinner somewhere in between, that, indeed, someday there will be silence. I am just not sure it will be golden.

To the Window

Julie Damerell
Wayland, New York

My eyes bore into the page, furiously urging the words to leap up and quiet the one-year-old voice at my side. Hours spent cajoling, caressing, cooking, and cleaning have dried the well. But this short boy won't be ignored.

The kitty is missing.

He is frantic, his bleats of "kitty" rising in pitch and demand. Brown eyes plead with his still new voice. Then a chubby hand wraps around my index finger, and my resolve to steal a few minutes away melts.

Certain that my eyes will see what his cannot, he tugs at my finger, pulling all the way to my heart. This isn't the first time his will takes me where I would not otherwise go—to the window.

Kitty doesn't appear for me either, though meows tell me she's near. I see what he cannot name. The lawn sloping downhill to the fence of the horse farm, the young trees struggling to grow despite the wind that threatens their stand, the road winding down our hill and back up another in the distance. Today I can even see beyond the horizon.

And I see what he cannot. Under sunnier skies, he will race around that lawn, gleefully chasing the kitty and balls and butterflies. I will be close behind, struggling to hold on to that which demands to be free—him. Together we'll note the trees' first buds and last leaves, marking time. As nature compels their growth and change every season, so it will the toddler by my side. That winding road will carry him away. I can see what he cannot—the future.

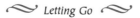

He won't remember my finger in his hand today, but I will, knowing it helped him find his way.

*S*nap-Shots

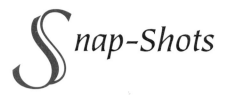

Judith Price
Wynnewood, Pennsylvania

Sometimes I turn around expecting to see a familiar face or to touch a familiar hand or hear a familiar voice when the curtain drops and time and images blur.

The picture of an infant restless in a car seat fades out as the view of an adolescent eager to take the wheel crystallizes and the shutter in my mind's eye clicks, focusing on a bicycle disappearing down the block.

The picture of a toddler, hesitant at the top step, fades out as the image of a teenager anxious to depart with college dreams comes into focus. Leap into soccer teams and summer camp.

The picture of fears calmed with special blankets fades out as the memories of dilemmas solved only by long-distance calls replaces tears dried with Popsicles and cartoon Band-Aids.

Past, future, present. Inner snap-shots assembled from a mother's memories.

*H*igh Chair Procrastination

Roberta Proctor
Coral Gables, Florida

It took me forever to buy a high chair. I was looking for a good price because, as a single mother staying home with my baby until I complete my degree, I need to conserve every penny. So, from the beginning, I decided not to rush the process. I answered ads in the local sales flyer and visited homes to check out used high chairs, but they looked so sad and spotted sitting in garages and kitchen corners. Then I tackled the discount stores where, in contrast to the used ones, the display chairs gleamed newly on shoulder-high, angled shelves. Tipped forward, with trays jutting out like petulant lips, they taunted me to touch, to buy.

On a trip to the toy store I even brought my son, Nathan, a week shy of seven months, and let him try out some of the chairs. I had fun watching him bang on the trays, the kind of fun mothers have waving as their children spin by on carnival rides—a temporary fun—fun they leave behind with the candy and carnies for the dark drive home. It didn't feel to me, even seeing Nathan grinning at me with his two new teeth, that the high chair was an inevitability. So, we drove home, Nathan sleeping in his car seat, my thoughts moving easily on to other things.

Without saying so outright, my mother recognized that my comparison shopping was really stalling. One weekday afternoon about three, she called me up to tell me there was a high chair at a local consignment shop. "It's only thirty-five dollars," she said, "so if there's nothing wrong with it and it looks okay, I'd like you to pick it up for me. You know, so he'll have one over here, too."

I agreed without hesitation. I'm always looking for a way to save my mom a few steps or a few dollars, especially considering how supportive she's always been of me. So, I drove Nathan over there, liked the high chair and quickly made my purchase. When I reached my mother's house, I was too busy settling Nathan into his playpen and washing down the new chair to comprehend what seed of change my mother had planted in me. She knew what she was doing. She knew that once I actually went out and bought a high chair, even if it was for her, it would be easier to buy one for myself.

The next night, she stayed with Nathan while I went out to buy a high chair for my apartment. I found one easily. It was only as I sat on the living room floor assembling it that I came to terms with my earlier resistance.

As I recalled Nathan's first-time desire to nurse in the bath a few hours ago, I was overcome by a fondness for the precious months of breast-feeding we have shared, the dusky night feedings. I feared the change in our nursing relationship that eating represented. The purchase of a high chair ushered in a new era.

Eating symbolized, for me, the beginning of Nathan's independence. Even though he won't stop nursing tomorrow, or next week, or next month, he eventually will stop. Just as he eventually will stop doing a lot of the things I enjoy so much about his infancy. As he changes, I will change, too; mothering a walking, talking child will seem completely unlike mothering an infant. But as I practiced positioning the tray in its various slots, I knew that this was the way of life: incessant change. You can't step into the same river twice, Heraclitus told us, and with motherhood, it's even more true. It is the only journey I've ever experienced during which, in the evening, I can already feel nostalgic about something that happened that afternoon. Everything happens so fast.

First Rock

Julie Damerell
Wayland, New York

Cool enough to cover easily skinned knees but warm enough for a bare head, fall is a mother's dream season. Mother Nature's house is strewn with colorful cast-offs. Her leaves, like my children's toys and socks and shoes, have to be picked up again and again and again. A messy house isn't ugly cluttered, it is simply our home's most natural state.

Before "mommy" meant me, mine was a passing familiarity with fall's chaotic beauty. Years from jumping in piles of leaves, nature charmed me from a friendly distance. Now my children's nearness to our footworn path draws me closer. For them I sacrifice my lawn chair, kneeling and sitting on the ground.

Rusty pine needles serve as my uneasy cushion there. Mother Nature's touch, like mine, is roughened by her work. Yet, I am her prodigal daughter. For me, she has decorated today in glory.

I squirm and return the gaze of Riley, the squirrel boy. At one, less conditioned by time and space off the ground, he delights in nature up close. Storing animal crackers in his cheeks, he wordlessly implores me to supply more despite the vanilla ooze seeping from the corners of his mouth.

Scampering toward me, he climbs up to wrap his arms around my neck and rest his head on my shoulder. Brief glimpses of squirrels in the woods bordering our yard catch my eye. It won't be many years before, like them, he'll scurry away from me to hide treasures. Today will be just another brief glimpse of the future.

Earlier he brought me a rock, his first. A misshapen oblong, pocked-granite gift, it was hoary with lines and unexpected angles, like a finger crooked with age.

I'd tossed his golden handfuls of grass. Surely this more solid present would stay. But I threw it a few feet for his sister to retrieve, which she did, and then a few more, daring her to find it again.

Time seems endless, rocks seem permanent. Both disappear. I saw Riley's rock as one of hundreds he might hand me in a lifetime and let go just as easily as the wind ran with his grassy gifts. Eyes can betray the heart. Mine told me, too late, that this rock was a keeper.

Today's sweet breeze urged the steady return of the leaves to the Earth, making trees barely splendid. Like the autumn breeze, four-year-old sisters are persistent. Colleen found the rock, along with three others.

A rock in hand is a memory captured. Colleen's smooth stones will remind me of my unexpected delight with her travels into the world, away from me, into her own joy. She is the leaf caught in the breeze and I am the sturdy, swaying tree behind her dancing journey. Riley does not roam as far. He is the acorn still nestled in my shade. His rock will beckon me over time, reminding me of an eager, almost tripping crawl, walnut eyes demanding my pleasure, and a small, too big hand offering me his treasure.

This pudgy boy and his lanky sister are treasures, too, keepers from the start. Memories gather like falling leaves, each one less distinct because of the others. I will save more rocks.

The Tobacco Stick

Priscilla J. Harris
Harrodsburg, Kentucky

He carries a tobacco stick. He's almost as tall as I am, which isn't saying much. He just turned nine, but he can't wait to surpass me. He walks proud, stepping high, head up, back straight, using the stick as if he needs it. The dog stays close by his side, as dogs are wont to do. A boy should have a dog.

He checks the livestock's watering trough. He pokes at it with his stick and pushes his hands down in the coolness of the water, then wipes his dripping hands on his pants. He climbs one plank up on the fence looking, thinking, dreaming, scheming, and surveying the place. Suddenly I see how swiftly these nine years have passed, and that when only nine more are gone, he likely will be too.

That is when I'll long to be that tobacco stick even as he towers over me. I hope he'll still walk proud, stepping high with his head up and his back straight, holding on to that tobacco stick as if he needs it.

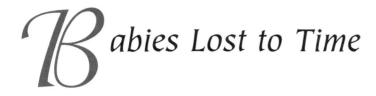

Babies Lost to Time

Susan Whitehouse
Lexington, Kentucky

I polished baby cups this morning. I saw bumps from falls, dents from teeth. I remembered smiles, boisterous hands that clapped, threw, pounded, rubbed sleepy eyes, patted cheeks, and held my hand.

I felt a tear trickle for babies lost to time, to adulthood. And then I smiled.

My Second and My Last

Moryt Milo
Campbell, California

When I hold my nineteen-month-old son in my arms, nothing feels more important. My priorities seem to fall into place and everything else in the world seems greatly reduced in value.

It's 9:30 at night. I go in to check on my son. Thinking he is asleep, I look down into his crib and I am surprised to see this innocent little soul lying on his back smiling at me. He is staring at me with his huge, blue eyes, expressing a trust only a child knows. Once my eyes have adjusted to the darkness I see that he has pulled off his no-skid socks. One is lying haphazardly by his side, the other clutched in his mouth and hands. It is a rather comical sight. I am selfishly glad that he is still awake and doesn't yet follow all the bedtime rules. As I pick him up, that magical sensation of his head nuzzling in the nape of my neck takes over. His little body molds into that familiar position. We sit in the rocking chair and silently glide back and forth.

I seem to feel these moments quietly slipping away. With each "first" I experience a bit of sadness mixed with the joy. I find myself cherishing every minute. I remind myself not to take any of it for granted.

As we rock in the silence of the night, I feel as if I am meditating and comforting my own soul as much as I am soothing his. Quietly, slowly, I hear his rhythmic breathing take hold. I know it is this unspoken closeness that gently puts him to sleep.

It is time to carry him back to his crib. But just one more minute please. I close my eyes and rock him for just a little longer. For I know he is my second and my last child.

# This Dawn

Gloria Watson
Bloomington, Minnesota

He wakes coughing, frightened by the still unfamiliar silence even though he has had his own room for four months. Awakened, I don't curse with the usual words that sometimes accompany his name during the wee hours. This dawn, I feel good about finding my way to his room.

"I can't sleep." Blond hair shimmers in the blind-filtered street light. I bend toward it. I feel for him in the darkness.

"It's okay. Mom's here." My mouth brushes his hair. "Are you thirsty?"

"No, but will you cuddle with me a little while?"

I slide into his cave of covers and smell his familiar little boy scent. He turns backside towards my cavern. One arm wraps around him. He says, "Both arms. I want both arms around me."

I imagine twenty years beyond this moment. I think of this flaxen head. This small, strong body large enough to wrap his arms around someone else. Hold tight! Kiss the soft nape of his neck! Can't he stay my little boy forever?

When Did This Happen?

Sue Poli
Clementon, New Jersey

He lies sleeping at 7:30 A.M. We always have to wake him for school. When did this happen? Many a morning, at 4:30, 5:00, certainly by 6:00, we'd hear the dreaded badum, badum as he jumped from his bed to tumble between us with a book. "Read, Mom." How I resented my lost sleep.

He's been in his room for an hour playing. When did this happen? He was always underfoot, deep in toy-car fantasy. Supper was cooked amid racing cars and construction zones, a minefield to negotiate with a pot of hot soup. Plunking down in my favorite chair meant a lapful of boy and books. A telephone call was an invitation to play with some forbidden item or climb to the highest cabinet. Now he plays alone in another part of the house not wishing to be disturbed.

Those first stress-filled, labor-intensive years have been replaced by a peaceful rhythm that affords me periods of privacy and periods of companionship, times to take pride in his independence and others to relish being needed. I must not be deluded into believing that this will last forever or even until tomorrow. It's my first time around in this job. I can't anticipate what is ahead, but I sure can appreciate today.

The Tooth Fairy

Mary Francine Crawley
Davis, California

As a full-time mother of four and a part-time dental hygienist, I find that one of my hardest jobs of all is that of being the tooth fairy, especially with our two sets of bunk beds. I finally started using the envelope system and it made my life a lot easier, especially since a large envelope keeps a tooth safe under a pillow and is easy for me to find.

As my oldest son approached twelve years old, and was still losing teeth, he would ask me, "Is this a good spot to put the envelope under my pillow, Mom?" Then he would give me a knowing smile to confirm what I already knew. He was on to this tooth fairy thing, but he was willing to keep it a secret because well, money is money, and this was easy money!

I still remember the hectic morning that Patrick lost his first tooth. He was almost the last person in his first-grade class to lose a tooth and so it was a day that we had all been anxiously awaiting. This particular morning, however, we woke up late, had dry cereal and rushed out the door for school. He tried to tell me several times, but I put him off by explaining that whatever it was would have to wait until later! I was in a hurry to drop everyone at school and get to the airport to pick up Grandma and Grandpa that day. So, when I did pick him up after school and heard of the momentous event that occurred that morning I felt bad that I hadn't taken the time to listen. I asked him then, "Well, Patrick, where is your tooth?" He looked up at me and answered, "I ate it for breakfast."

Meghan was almost six years old when she lost her first tooth. Ironically, she lost it right in front of her dentist, my boss of four years. She was showing him how far she could push the tooth with her tongue when it came flying out of her mouth.

Amanda, our third child, caught on pretty fast to the fact that losing teeth meant money. She started using her tongue to push on her teeth and lost her first tooth while still in preschool. The day she felt that first wiggly tooth she exclaimed joyfully, "This is the best day of my life!" A few weeks later, we heard a "crunching" sound at dinner and out came another tooth. She again exclaimed, "This is the best day of my life!" The next day, after finding the money under her pillow, she made the same statement a third time.

Now, her older sister, having had just about enough of this best-day-of-my-life stuff, reminded Amanda, "I thought you said the best day was the day your tooth first wiggled."

Amanda slowly turned to her and replied, "It's like I keep telling you, Meghan, the days just keep getting better and better."

Well, I continue to be the tooth fairy at our house where my youngest son, Danny, is still waiting for his first loose tooth. I haven't been caught red-handed yet, although on certain occasions I have forgotten to do my duty. And the days, well, they just keep getting better.

$\mathcal{B}$ittersweet

Judy Schaaf
Minneapolis, Minnesota

My fourteen-year-old daughter, Laura, bolts out of the house, swings the door open, and defiantly declares, "Don't expect me back before noon tomorrow." She yanks the door shut, just short of breaking the "no slamming doors" rule.

Thirteen-year-old Ben slouches over with both hands deep in his pockets and stumbles out. "I'll be at Pete's," he mumbles, closing the door behind him.

I stand in the middle of the living room needing something to lean on but unable to move. There are no mindless tasks that are compelling enough to push me to action. Usually the house is much too small for all that is going on, but now the house feels hollow. Ten years ago I would have traded a year of my life to have three hours by myself in my own home. Today I need to escape.

I head out on foot for Linden Hills and its many coffee houses and decide on Sebastian Joe's, where the ambiance encourages lingering. I do my best thinking in crowded places, where anonymity helps me to focus and put my thoughts in proper perspective.

At the entrance, I grab the door for a mother struggling to maneuver a double stroller. I picture Ben in the backpack and Laura in the stroller as I drag them up and down steps, escalators, and unramped curbs, attempting to be as independent as I can be with a temper-tantrum-prone toddler and a four-month-old with irregular sleep patterns.

I suddenly find myself at the front of the line. I splurge on an extra large cappuccino, and find a table for one in a remote corner of the patio. The young mom navigates her stroller through an obstacle course of tables and chairs and legs and plants and garbage cans and recycling bins, until she reaches her destination.

A woman in a straight red skirt and matching jacket greets her with a huge smile and open arms. She exclaims in the direction of the baby, "Oh, she's so beautiful!" Eventually, she turns to the toddler and cheerfully asks, "How do you like your new sister?"

The toddler runs over to Mom and clutches her kneecap. A rush of newborn memories floods my mind. As a sensitive, empathetic, thirty-five-year-old, I thought that I had experienced a wide range of emotions, but nothing prepared me for the all-encompassing intensity of my first year as a mother. After giving birth, I was overwhelmed by the responsibility, as well as amazed by the miracle of my daughter's existence. Every bone in my body ached with exhaustion, but I was unable to close my burning eyes during the long-awaited nap times. Pacing and pacing with my inconsolable daughter brought tears of despair, soon followed by tears of joy as she lay cradled in my arms. A daytime household in turmoil from baby paraphernalia and unfinished tasks was transformed at bedtime into a peaceful portrait of Madonna and Child. One day I felt like an inanimate milk machine. The next day I was in awe of my life-sustaining function. I alternated days of feeling clumsy, confused, and incompetent, with days of feeling confident and all-knowing. I was overcome by personal insecurity and vulnerability while proudly creating complete security for my baby.

On the patio, a piercing scream causes heads to turn toward Mom. She paces around the ice cream table with her baby on her shoulder, pulling out books, action figures, and toy cars for the toddler. Occasionally she looks up and responds to her friend. The crying subsides as the baby disappears under Mom's sweatshirt and finds her food source. The toddler pleads monotonously, "Go home, go home, go home," as he burrows into her already occupied lap. The friend's smile freezes as she attempts to continue the conversation.

In another life, I thought parents had more control over their children's personalities—environment over heredity, nurture over nature. But Laura cried throughout most of her first year. As intensely as she cried, she also beamed and babbled with ecstasy, but Mom or Dad always needed to be within arm's length. To this day, she experiences everything intensely, and she still prefers a parent with her when facing new situations. Being the first-born child of a mother who also was first born, she shares my irritating and compulsive perfectionism. It has been a painful experience to watch my child struggle with my lifelong battles.

Ben came into the world as if from different parents. He has always been quiet and pensive. I took him anywhere, anytime. Ben never had stranger anxiety, he was comfortable being held by just about anyone. He ate what he should, when he should, and how he should. I needed to have Ben to feel I was a competent parent.

The toddler's whining escalates to shrieks of, "Go home!" His face flushes near-purple. He flails arms and legs at his mother. The patio audience attempts to continue its own conversations, with only occasional glances. As the friend stiffly bounces the baby on her knees, Mom grabs the impatient toddler and a little too firmly forces him into the stroller. With the baby safe in the stroller, Mom makes her escape.

As she scurries past my table I tap her arm, look at her flushed face framed by damp strands of hair, and attempt to reassure her, "It gets easier." She shakes her auburn head and rolls her eyes. She looks back to her friend through a cheerful façade, "I'll get a sitter. We can have lunch." Realistically, she should say, "I'll see you in about six years."

Blissfully pregnant fourteen years ago, I was absolutely sure my child would never have created such a scene. I was going to be Earth Mother, carrying my child with me everywhere, nursing on demand until she was at least three. In reality, when Laura was a couple of months old, I was usually still in my bathrobe at 3:00 P.M. hoping to take a shower and eat something for lunch. I yearned for a

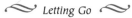

job to go to, fantasizing about a boring desk job with a bathroom that got cleaned, a desk that was organized, and an uninterrupted half-hour lunch break. I experienced a loss of a dream that year—the dream of what kind of children I would have, and of what kind of parent I would become.

Walking home past the Linden Hills playground, I notice Mom sitting in a sunny spot on the wooden bench. Her eyes are closed, her face raised toward the sun, her hair gently blowing across her face. The baby is asleep on her shoulder and the toddler passed out in the stroller. An elderly couple walks by with many years of experience imprinted on their faces and in their posture. Feeling obligated to give advice, they warn her, "Enjoy these years. They go so fast." Mom smiles politely.

I haven't forgotten the struggles of those early years. I am still waiting for a time when parenting isn't such a struggle. Instead, it has been a continuous journey of emotional extremes—exuberant joy and excruciating pain, magnificent pride and overwhelming frustration, passionate love and intense anger. But it is a journey I would not have missed, for the challenges have brought rewards as well. As Laura's relentless struggle for independence reminds me, they will be gone before long, and I will feel compelled to advise young mothers to enjoy these years because they will pass too quickly.

As I slide in the back door of the house, Laura bounds into the kitchen. "Mom, Jessica's Dad is taking us to the mall and can you iron my denim shirt and can I have my allowance a little early?"

We look into each other's hazel eyes. She lays her head down on my shoulder and wraps her arms around my waist while I envelop her shoulders. "Thanks, Mom. I love you."

View from an Empty Nest

Lana Stone
Stillwater, Oklahoma

Wiggly one sitting on your mother's lap squirming to break free, I see you and recall my own shiny-faced boy with the coppery curls of twenty years past. Now grown, he nearly ran me ragged!

He never walked if he could zoom like a car from place to place. "Vrrroomm, vrrroomm," he would say. I knew when he'd arrived by the squeal of his brakes.

Parked at the kitchen cupboards he'd become a one-man band. The crash of pot-lid cymbals and wooden spoons on metal pans were music to his untrained ears. I had to keep mine covered. He was always into everything. A tireless explorer of electrical cords and stereo systems, vacuum cleaners and mowers. I don't think I relaxed until he was ten.

Wiggly one sitting on your mother's lap squirming to break free, I see you and recall my own shiny-faced boy with the coppery curls and what I wouldn't give just to hold him again for a minute, my little boy, now grown.

When I Leave Them

Minneapolis, Minnesota

My theory of child-rearing as it applied to post-high-school children was fairly simple: I believed that a college education, preferably in another city or state, was the ideal first step to independent adulthood. I wanted that for my daughters and I worked very hard to provide it. I had an opportunity to put my theory into practice.

One day, my husband, our oldest daughter, and I drove from Minneapolis to Chicago. The drive was pleasant and we enjoyed being together, just the three of us, since her younger sisters were at home with Grandma and Grandpa. I was happy about the college she had chosen, I was excited for her, and I was very proud of her. I had no regrets that she was leaving home. I was really taking it quite well!

We helped her move into her dorm room, had dinner in the dining hall with her, went to the parents' meetings, and then went to our motel. She stayed in the dorm. The next morning she got registered for classes, got her books, and helped a high school friend move into a room in the same dorm. My husband and I did the rest of the "parent things," had lunch with our daughter, and then prepared to return to Minneapolis.

My husband had planned a special trip home for the two of us. We were going to drive home via Highway 12 instead of taking the interstate. We had driven that route many, many times during our early years together and he wanted to take it again. He had some places where he wanted to stop. We were going to take our time—a romantic, nostalgic time together.

144   ∼ *Mother Voices* ∼

Then it happened. Our daughter walked out to the car to say good-bye. After she hugged us both she turned around, put her hands in her pockets, sort of hunched her shoulders up, and walked away. I don't think I'll ever forget that picture of her. At that moment I completely "lost it." It was as if I were deserting my child. I started to cry and I couldn't stop. We drove away and I kept crying. Two hours later we found a motel and I got ready for bed. I was still crying. I cried myself to sleep and the next morning I cried some more. We had breakfast in silence because I couldn't carry on a conversation without getting weepy.

Our first stop was in Baraboo, Wisconsin, to see the Circus Museum. When we got out of the car, I realized that I didn't have my purse. We drove (over an hour) back to our breakfast restaurant to retrieve it. By this time, my husband had given up. I wasn't any fun and neither of us were enjoying ourselves. We got on the interstate and were in Minneapolis before dinner.

I still remember that day with tears. All of my children have left home. Two are married and have children of their own. Two have lived for a time in other countries, on other continents. When they leave me, I miss them, but it seems normal and my heart doesn't break. But when I leave them, even when I leave them in their own homes, I feel this awful "pang" and tears come. It makes no sense. I wonder how old they and I will have to be before I can leave them without feeling as if I am deserting them.

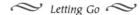 *Letting Go*

Go West, Young Man

Patricia P. Miller
Williamston, Michigan

Young men have been heading "west" since our continent was discovered. The lure of new lands, mountains, and open space has tugged at the minds and hearts of countless young adventurers. Tired of home, ready for new experiences, and hearing the siren song of the western frontier calling, teary-eyed wives, lovers, and mothers waved farewell as their husbands and sons departed into the setting sun, its rays beaming hopes and dreams deep into their souls.

My son, Tristan, muddled through a sour high school experience and was working as a landscaper and handyman, rejecting the college-bound ethic of family and friends. I had raised him and his two sisters, one older and one younger, since a painful divorce ten years earlier. His one great joy in life was skiing, a difficult sport to pursue in central Ohio and an expensive pastime, as well. The one dream he shared with me among the many lurking in the shadowy recesses of his adolescent mind was to ski, to go "out west," to go to school and be able to ski in the mountains.

I wanted desperately to get him motivated and into college, so we began to plan how he might actually do this. The plan was to start with one course at the community college; he was scared and doubted his ability to do college work. He tried a math course since he had done well in high school math. Lots of jitters and sweaty palms later, he completed the course with an "A." What a great day!

He took more courses and as his confidence grew, he began to write to colleges in Colorado, land of dreams. The day his acceptance came from Colorado State, he was ecstatic. His dream to go west was coming true. Darker thoughts invaded my mind: how would I pay for this, how could I watch him leave home, probably never really to return?

Launching an independent person, a child ready to seek and find his place in the adult world, is every parent's primary job. The baby I once held is now leaving me, the son I relied upon for "male" things is going too, and I must not only accept this, I must encourage and help plan it.

As moving-out day approached, a sadness I had never experienced crept into our home, lingering over our "last trip to the store," our "last dinner together," mocking the innocence of his small white cat, curled contentedly in his lap unsuspecting of the loss to come. But like all good mothers, I encouraged him, helped him pack, bought him new clothes, petted the cat knowing soon she would be all that remained of him at home, except the memories—except the pride and love I have for him.

There were tears the evening before he left, falling on the white cat's back as I said good night, not good-bye. He was leaving at noon the next day, heading west, to find his own life and dreams. I paid only scant attention at work the next day, my mind on my son and his departure.

But wings are designed for flight, and the birds that soar highest take the largest first step over the edge. Parents must give their children the tools to fly, that ultimate chance that life offers to become unique individuals and live out their own visions of happy lives.

As long as there is a "west," young adventurers will be called and will go. As parents, we smile and wave, we encourage and support, and we cry after they are down the drive and around the corner. They're bittersweet tears, of pride as well as sadness and loss. It's a mirror of the journey through life traveled by us all.

Letting Go

Just Call Me Dysfunctional

Lynne L. Wisman
Mason City, Iowa

It was there, hidden beneath storage boxes, old school yearbooks, and drawings saved from elementary school, that I found the stack of memories. Tied with a lime-green shoelace from an old track shoe, the odd assortment of Valentines, Mother's Day cards, and birthday messages waiting to be rediscovered. The pile of cards smelled of mildew and were yellowed by age, but the messages were the same. Testimonials of love, signed by little girl and boy hands, dotted with x's and o's; sweet words reaching out from the past, evoking more emotions today than they had yesterday. I felt as though I had rediscovered something I once had, if only for a moment.

They were good years that evaporated like a ghost in the night. The children grew taller, older, smarter, and more independent with each passing day. They were growing up; we were growing old. We were happy then, a normal, loving, well-adjusted, typical American family, at least according to my standards.

The children are gone now...from our home, our refrigerator, our cars and our wallets, but they'll never be gone from our hearts. Time has passed and they have changed. So have we, for no one ever stays the same. In place of children are adults, the benefactors of wonderful memories, a sea of tears, a wealth of good times, bad times, laughter, heartbreak, and pride. All the result of a "normal" family life. Right?

Wrong.

Our daughter recently announced she is in therapy to heal the "inner child" from damage inflicted by a dysfunctional family life.

Oh. Really? This isn't a joke? Your therapist said we are a dysfunctional family? But, but...(sputter) you were born into a family who loves you more than you'll ever know. You had a wonderful childhood, family vacations, religious training, and nice clothing. Your friends were always welcome in our home. We supported and encouraged all of your dreams.

You were given a car that you destroyed. We then provided you with another, because everyone deserves a second chance. We educated you beyond high school at our expense. When you announced you were getting married, we paid for a beautiful wedding. Then you announced you were getting divorced, for the "most wonderful man in the world" had, according to you, become as "stubborn and ornery as a hog in a sweet corn patch." We suggested you pay for that transaction yourself.

Now, which part of your life has been dysfunctional and whose fault do you think it might be? A decent home and loving parents doesn't guarantee a perfect life...or even a happy one. Do you actually believe we are a dysfunctional family?

Well, on second thought...perhaps we are. We didn't become dysfunctional, however, until three healthy teenagers rendered us nearly insane. Three stereos cranked to the max playing three different tapes eighteen hours a day may have created a permanent neurological deficit where one didn't previously exist.

Or perhaps it was the vast number of telephone calls that conveniently overflowed onto our line when the teen phone wasn't sufficient to handle all of your personal calls. We were genuinely amazed at your ability to carry on two different conversations on separate lines at the same time.

Perhaps you can recall the Christmas at Gramma's when you were thirteen? That was the year an eighth-grade boy gave you a pair of bikini panties with "Tunnel of Love" stamped on the crotch. Grandmother was younger then, but she nearly had a heart attack. So did your father and I. That was the same year your brother announced he was going to marry Becky. They were in ninth grade. We found it difficult to be at three different athletic events at once, but one of us was always there to see you compete. And we also found it difficult to afford the

beautiful clothing the three of you wore to homecoming, the Valentine's dance, and prom. The dresses are still in storage bags in a downstairs closet with the other treasures you don't have room for in your own home.

The shifting array of young people and stray animals the three of you brought home prompted us to buy a twenty-two-cubic-foot freezer, a cow and eight pigs that would eventually wind up on the dining room table. We liked the wood sign your brother carved for us at the county fair the year he was seventeen. "Wisman's Community Kitchen" hung on the wall over the chairs his friends occupied at meals until he left for eight years of college...without Becky, Mindy, Sara, Julie, and Kathy.

We remodeled the kitchen the year your younger sister graduated and left home for bright lights and city nights, a life free of parental supervision and concerned lectures. Your father and I were alone at last...with nothing but memories of all those wonderful years, several thousand dollars in college tuition to be paid, and two weddings waiting in the wings.

When real life became too emotionally demanding and there wasn't anywhere to turn, you moved back in. Your psychological baggage was far heavier than your material belongings but we dealt with it to the best of our ability until you were strong enough to get on with your life. If I recall correctly, your sister moved back home the day you moved out. Her psychological baggage had become heavy, too. But it was alright because loving and helping each other is what families are all about.

It seems like a long time ago, and it was a long time ago. I still get Valentine's and Mother's Day cards. They come from far-away places, quickly signed and dropped in a postal box. Sometimes a photograph of our grandchildren accompanies the card, reminding me of many things...my own mortality, how much I dislike the distance that separates me from those I love so much, how little I once knew about loving and missing people we have in our lives...but don't really have at all. It has been hard to learn those lessons.

How Did You Do it, Mom?

Katie Grev
Austin, Minnesota

Chad came into the kitchen where I was stirring up orange juice. It was close to midnight and the next item on my agenda was getting to bed. However, glancing at my son I saw a look in his eyes that said he wanted to talk. I placed the juice in the refrigerator and sat down at the round oak table pretending to arrange some papers.

At nineteen years of age, Chad is a slender six-foot-two. A wave of sentimental memories hits me: my toddler in soft blue flannel pajamas, the little boy who ran his toy cars up and down me as if I were a car ramp, the adolescent who hung GI Joes from the ceiling fan on reconnaissance missions.

He leaned up against the kitchen counter, stretching his long tanned legs out into the small kitchen. "Mom, remember the time we went swimming at Woods Lake and when it was time to go home, Kris and I came right out of the water as soon as you called us, but Chip and Melanie ignored their mother's calls?"

"Mm-hmmm."

"And I heard lots of my friends talk back to their parents, even swear at them?"

I nodded.

"Mom, you should write a book or something on how you raised us kids. We've never talked back to you or Dad. We get along well. How did you do it?"

We talked 'til the wee hours that night. We talked of respect, treating children as worthwhile human beings; of listening to meanings behind words and actions; of an abundance of hands-on affection and a minimum of hands-on discipline. We talked of enjoying children and harmony between parents; of a large quantity

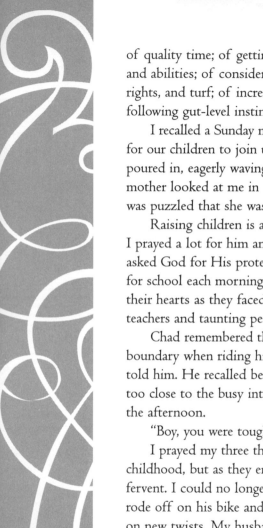

of quality time; of getting to know each other and encouraging personal dreams and abilities; of consideration toward each family member—respecting privacy, rights, and turf; of increasing freedom and responsibility with maturity; and of following gut-level instinct instead of professionally established rules.

I recalled a Sunday morning waiting with other mothers in the church sanctuary for our children to join us for service. When the door opened and the children poured in, eagerly waving their Sunday school papers and projects, another young mother looked at me in astonishment, "You seem so happy to see your kids!" I was puzzled that she was astonished. Of course I was happy to see my kids!

Raising children is an awesome responsibility and I revealed a secret to Chad: I prayed a lot for him and his sisters, Debbie and Kris, through those years. I asked God for His protective hand over my children as they walked out the door for school each morning. I asked for physical protection, for a shield around their hearts as they faced the challenges and hurts of sometimes unfair, uncaring teachers and taunting peers.

Chad remembered the chalk line I drew on the sidewalk on Eighth Street; his boundary when riding his Green Machine, "You can go this far and no farther," I told him. He recalled being grounded at age four. He'd gone past the chalk line, too close to the busy intersection, and had to stay in the yard for the remainder of the afternoon.

"Boy, you were tough, Mom," he said with a twinkle in his hazel eyes.

I prayed my three through the cuts and scrapes and bumps and bruises of childhood, but as they entered their teenage years, my prayers became more fervent. I could no longer protect Chad with a chalk line on the sidewalk as he rode off on his bike and eventually drove away in the family car. Parenting took on new twists. My husband and I made some mistakes; the kids sometimes made poor choices. Through it all, we loved them and continued to pray.

Three weeks ago, Chad came home from his freshman year at Augustana College, his battered old Ford Capri loaded with nine months of college living.

As he turned onto Eighth Street, he saw me shakily skating on my new roller blades. Pulling up beside me, he rolled down the window and hollered, "Hey, lady! You're grounded! You went past the chalk line!"

As my husband and I begin this new stage in our lives, watching our children enter adulthood, Chad's words often come back to me, "How did you do it, Mom? Someday I'll want to raise my children the way I was raised," and I realize that this is the highest compliment a mother could receive.

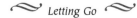 *Letting Go*

$\mathcal{L}$etting Go

Sally Witmer Ehlert
West Des Moines, Iowa

I am writing memories today in this old baby book, and my "baby" is twenty years old!

Could it be I'm slow at letting go? When she was sick that day at college, I wanted so much to take her ginger ale and chicken soup.

At Christmas time I hang her stocking over the fireplace, and find it already filled with memories. When she's home to visit, I still want to know where she's going, with whom, and what time she'll be home. I care and I'm slow at letting go.

Someone very special to her shares her day-to-day life now, and holds knowledge of her that was once mine. It hurts just a little, this letting go.

Special Circumstances

Mommy, When Will I Be Stronger

Rosemary C. Jurman
Rochester, New York

It was a warm morning in July as Daniel, my three-year-old, and I walked to a neighbor's house. I was taking care of a friend's baby for the day, and Daniel cheerfully helped me push the stroller as we made our way down the street. He serenaded baby Emily with his favorite train song, her feet bouncing in happy appreciation. By the time he finished the last verse of, "Train Is A-Coming," we were at Jennifer's door.

I had only known her for a few months, but we had become fast friends. Both at-home mothers with young children, we always seemed to have something to talk about. When we got there, her kids were outside playing with a neighbor's children, and naturally Daniel wanted to join them. Through the back screen door I watched them play, and seeing an unfamiliar face, thought, "Maybe Daniel will make a new friend today."

Daniel is small, slight for his age. Due to his low muscle tone, his strength, balance, and coordination are not what they should be. So I keep an extra eye on him, especially when he's outside. I continued to watch them for a short while longer; Daniel was seemingly quite content as he played with a ride-on toy. Then I directed my attention to the baby and Jennifer, who was getting us some cold drinks. As we talked, I heard some shouting from outside.

"You're smaller! We're bigger than you! We're stronger!"

"They can't be talking about Daniel," I thought. "We've only been here a few minutes, and these kids hardly know him." I glanced out the door and saw Daniel standing alone, the other children in a semicircle around him. He stood as if

frozen. A scene from *Lord of The Flies* flashed through my mind. My first instinct was to go out there, but something told me to stay put and see how he would handle it, knowing I wouldn't always be there to protect him.

The children continued their jeers. One of the boys, perhaps a year older than Daniel, suddenly ran up to him and began twisting his arm. Daniel bit his lip and remained motionless. At this point, fearing for his safety, I bolted out the door. The boy immediately let go of Daniel, and I spoke to them in the scolding voice a good mother rarely uses. It mattered little to me that I wasn't their mother.

How dare they mistreat such a gentle-hearted boy, my son! "Stop that!" I shouted. "How would you like it if someone twisted your arm?" And remembering their taunts, I asked them accusingly, "What is bigger? What is stronger?" The children gave me blank stares. I could feel the heat in my face. "Some people are fatter, some are thinner, some are taller, some are shorter. But we are all people," I continued. "Everyone is different." Then turning to Daniel, I asked him if he was okay. He nodded his head yes. His eyes were flooded, but his cheeks were still dry.

I took his hand to go inside when he asked me, "Mommy, when will I be stronger?" This question was something I wasn't prepared for. In the back of my mind, this scenario wouldn't happen until grade school. Ideally, it would never come. It hurt to answer, yet I found one. "Someday," I said in a thick voice. "Someday you will be stronger." Of course I knew that this was a half-truth. It's true that he'll be stronger than he is now, but would he ever be as strong as his peers? That remains to be seen.

We began to gather our things and the baby to go. Jennifer didn't know what to say. She lamely suggested that we stay awhile longer; maybe the kids would play with Daniel. He went back into the yard without coaxing, but played by himself. None of the children approached him, nor he them. We left shortly after that. Daniel was now aware of his "differences," and things would never be the same. We made the long walk home in silence.

Please Don't Forget Me This Time, Daddy

Maribeth Weed
Rochester, New York

We have been ready since 9:00 A.M., up early to be ready. It is now 10:15. I am sitting here watching you as you try so hard to sit patiently. Waiting for your Knight in Shining Armor to arrive. I can see in your little face the embarrassment you feel, so I will say nothing, but we both know he is not coming.

Yes, we did as we always do, both you and I. We got up and got you ready. Why? Because we both hope each time that it will be true. Oh, my baby...how my heart aches for you. I have watched that anxious little face for so very long now. So many times, so many lies. I know deep inside he does not realize how he hurts you. Maybe if only once he had to see this little person wait with no words expressed, although, as your Mommy, I know inside the words are so clear...

"Please don't forget me this time, Daddy."

Of course, you'll never say them. I know, because, after all, we both want to believe in your Knight in Shining Armor. Yes, next time we'll be right back here again waiting and hoping, the both of us for two very different reasons. You because you love him unconditionally and me because I love you unconditionally.

Deciding to Go

Marianne Peel Forman
East Lansing, Michigan

What I remember about that day is the damp heat as I wrenched clover and weed stalks from the side of the house. My hands were bruised and torn from the rose bushes and their prickers. He came out the back door all puffed up and heaving at the chest, banging words into wet air, scolding my pulling of weeds, telling me I was an irresponsible mother. The kids were splashing in the wading pool in their shorts and diapers instead of their bathing suits.

He returned to the television, focused only on the basketball game.

I crashed into the house, fingers dripping dirt and stem and leaf, announcing that I was leaving to find an apartment. Digging through the paper pile I ferreted out the classifieds.

I hid in the bathroom with the columns promising home.

No privacy is allowed here. The door was slammed open by a fist and a finger that began to pound my chest, breaking me at the waist, his hands wrapped around my throat until I could not breathe. The starch of his beard pierced my cheek.

And the babies cried for their Mama just outside the door.

The Shattering

Judith F. Moriarty
Bethlehem, Connecticut

It was a sun-splashed Saturday in early summer, my favorite time of year. As I prepared supper, I watched a mother duck in the pond out back proudly parading her young. For the hundredth time, I couldn't help thinking how much more protective animals are towards their young than many humans.

We had moved to Connecticut a few years before, after our seafood business had failed. People were in no position to buy king crab, shrimp, or lobster when the steel mills and oil industries went bust in western Pennsylvania.

Life in rural America had a down-home simplicity to it. Our small town had no movie theaters, no video arcades, no gangs, and no crack houses. Few could afford cable, which meant that children's laughter echoed through our town parks and down shaded country lanes. People still whispered about "the murder" twenty-five years before when a woman shot her abusive husband. Present-day problems in this isolated valley were drunken drivers, an occasional bar brawl, or another hunter being shot accidentally.

Our children were not influenced by designer clothes or hundred-dollar sneakers. Parents worked hard in the factories and on local farms. They would have laughed at the foolishness of a sixty-dollar pair of blue jeans or food money being spent on arcade games. The children fished, camped in the woods, and caught fireflies far into the night. Simple things like roller skating, picnics, and bike riding still managed to amuse. With no malls, neighbors shopped at the few dozen stores downtown. If it wasn't there, you didn't need it.

As much as we hated to leave, the only means of economic survival was for my husband to return to the construction trade. Work was plentiful in New York City, so we moved to Connecticut, which was an easy commute.

We left a town of seven thousand for a city of one hundred and ten thousand. Gone forever was the peace of mountain mornings, farmers' markets, or band concerts in the town park. We soon found ourselves engulfed in a world of mammoth buildings, sprawling malls, frenzied thruways, and designer people. Everywhere, there were dire warnings concerning one's safety. From color-coordinated car clubs to guard dogs and razor wire, freedom seemed just another word.

We rented a home in the north part of the city far from the chaos of downtown. Here, beyond the parkway, homes were situated on four-acre lots. Nature centers, bike trails, and the city's reservoir surrounded by massive pines completed the illusion of perfect serenity and safety. Here we could imagine that we were back in the tranquil mountains of Pennsylvania.

It was 6:15 P.M. The mother duck had ushered her little ones to the safety of the far bank. I felt a slight tug of apprehension wondering what was keeping the kids. My youngest son and gangly, blonde-haired niece had left early in the afternoon for their favorite activity, a picnic in the woods. Busy with the laundry, I'd paid scant attention as they packed baggies with chips, raisins, and peanut butter sandwiches—stopping only to grab a handful of tapes and the cassette player, before, with a bang of the door, they were off.

My apprehension grew. Brian, a curly haired thirteen-year-old with intense blue eyes, could be relied on for his promptness. Always very studious and serious, I enjoyed seeing him laughing and carefree.

I smiled, remembering the one time that the school had called asking me to come in to discuss a serious problem. Hands folded across his chest, the principal sternly informed me that my son was guilty of extortion. I almost fell off the chair wondering how this eleven-year-old kid had gotten himself involved with the Mafia.

As it turned out, Brian was charging kids a quarter to ride the school bus. Relieved, I thought, "How typical." Always the astute entrepreneur, he was continually looking for a way to "make a buck." At five years old he checked out customers in our store, read the stock market reports, and computed complicated math in his head. I assured the principal that I'd immediately put an end to his newest venture. I was thankful, thinking he hadn't yet matched the antics of his older brother. Jerry, the exact opposite, with a "devil-may-care" attitude, had informed the nuns in first grade that he wanted his walking papers. He was too smart for school. It escalated from there. Jerry could be counted on for being late, but not Brian.

Then the phone rang.

Brian was sobbing incoherently about being attacked by a stranger in the woods. They'd run to a nearby college security office, could we hurry over. Being the weekend, there was only one guard on duty whom Brian informed me spoke little English. My husband and I raced for the car, reaching the school in record time. I was immediately enraged when I saw the children disheveled, with dirty, tear-stained faces, sitting at the curb. The guard was nowhere to be found. Trying to remain calm and in control while comforting them, I managed to get a disjointed statement and description from them.

They had been picnicking in the woods when a bearded man brandishing a club had forced them into an abandoned shed and ordered them to disrobe. He then proceeded to perform various lewd acts, warning them if they cooperated they would not be harmed.

Just then, sirens wailed as numerous police cars, rescue trucks, and ambulances raced up. The ensuing hours are a blur of emergency room staff, detectives, interviews, and the children searching books of mug shots. It's only after the crisis of the moment, when you've gained some semblance of sanity, that you realize how differently things should have been handled and what you should have said.

As a social worker, I'd been involved in many crises, but nothing prepared me for this. Every day, the media bears witness to catastrophic happenings. Each of

us experiences feelings of anger, guilt, hopelessness, or fear. None of these even approaches the shattering that takes place at the very core of your being when your child is violated and terrorized.

There's a magic in the innocence and joy of a child. They embrace each day with such wonderment and trust. Secret campsites, the first snowfall, fireflies in the night; all are a source of joy-filled discovery. A deranged pervert can steal all this in a moment of depravity.

Standing in the hospital corridor while doctors administered to the children, I watched as the detectives carefully bagged various pieces of evidence. Shirts, shoes, and blue jeans covered with semen were all dutifully marked. The remnants of the picnic, still sealed in baggies, lay amongst this sordid mess. One of the detectives came up to me and said, "If there's any good to realize out of all this, I have to tell you that usually the kids end up murdered."

As I stood there looking at those packages of good and evil so haphazardly thrown together, I felt a convulsing and tearing in a part of my being that I never knew existed. It was an earthquake of the greatest magnitude, shaking everything I'd valued or held dear. It was the roar of a tornado, the ripping of hurricane winds, and the melting inferno of a forest fire, all at once.

After hours at the hospital and hours more at the police station, the kids finally fell asleep tucked into sleeping bags on the living room floor. We had to check all the doors several times and leave on lights.

At 2:30 A.M., I called a rape crisis hotline. For two hours, a kind woman calmly helped me gain control. It was only then that I realized that the police were supposed to contact them when we were at the hospital.

The next morning, my son and niece related in detail the horror of what had happened. I had both of the children write down how they felt and we then did a composite sketch of the attacker. My son related how he had a chance, at one point, to escape, but decided to stay, thinking his cousin would be killed if he left.

I was overwhelmed by his unselfish love and amazing bravery. I told him that he had the stuff that heroes are made of.

That same morning my husband and I went door-to-door warning our neighbors and handing out a description of the man. I naturally assumed that this would be one of the first things to which the police would attend. I no longer assumed the logical, I just did it myself.

We invited the neighborhood kids in to help make posters. From the very beginning we made sure nothing was kept secret. Our children were the victims, they had no need to feel ashamed. Secretiveness only encourages violators to go on with their sickening deeds.

For a while, my son collected knives. Every noise in the night brought fear, every delivery man was suspect. The woods, once so magical, were now menacing. After a few months, we moved to a high-rise apartment building with a security guard. Finally, there was a semblance of peace, but at what cost?

My son is now a graduate student in photography. His photographs pull you into a world of desperation, decay, emptiness, abandonment, and isolation.

Ann Miller, a Swiss psychologist, defines the mistreatment of children as, "the greatest crime that one human being can commit against another, causing psychological deformation in the next generation." A fractured treasure can be deftly mended, but the artist can never restore the exquisite beauty of the original piece.

*P*hoto Album

April Burk
Archer, Florida

"It's not cancer," the doctor volunteers over the phone.

"Well, good," I answer, not quite relieved. "What is it then?"

"Dysplasia," he responds. It is not a new concept to me—several friends and relatives have it, so it doesn't immediately seem scary. I imagine having the turncoat cells frozen off my cervix in the doctor's office, and that will be that, life will go on. But the doctor wants to see me to discuss my options.

At my appointment, I learn that freezing is only performed in less severe cases. My cells are on the third level of a pre-cancerous state. They need to be destroyed before they progress. My options include laser surgery or a hysterectomy, which my doctor doesn't recommend.

Responding to my four-month-old daughter's big grins with a smile of his own, he says, "For you, I suggest laser-cone surgery, which gives you a ninety-eight percent chance of full recovery. And you can have more children if you want to." Sam and I haven't decided if we want another baby, but the possibility of losing the choice chills me. Surgery with general anesthesia is scheduled for the following week.

I've never been in the hospital other than when my daughter was born. Two percent chance that I won't recover—I imagine the awful possibilities: Sam left to raise a baby on his own, me not getting to see my daughter grow up, and Kayla not knowing me. I've heard that children have little or no memory of their first three years.

Kayla not remembering me? That I can do something about. Creating a photo album distracts me from obsessing about the looming surgery. It feels good to be doing rather than waiting to be done to. But I can't completely ignore the inner voice whispering, "Life is so good. I have a family to care for. I'm too young."

As I sort through pictures, I realize there are no records to immortalize some of my own childhood memories. I hold dear the day my mother and I experimented with a blender, fresh tomatoes, and Worcestershire sauce trying to create the perfect glass of tomato juice. I don't remember if we ever succeeded, but I do remember the fun we had, just the two of us, measuring and tasting. I also remember waiting on the sidewalk for my turn to take a ride in my father's bicycle basket. He pedaled me through the neighborhood and we shared stories from the day. The importance of quality time cannot be underestimated. I resolve to find some way to show Kayla every day that I treasure her.

The week passes quickly. I feel positive and calm. I think I've covered all the worst-case scenarios until the pre-admission clerk asks if I have a living will. Yes, unplug me. I smile, making light. She doesn't laugh. I am not allowed to eat or drink anything after midnight, not even a sip of water, which is difficult because breastfeeding leaves me really parched. We arrive at the hospital at nine in the morning, toting stroller and diaper bag. I change into the thin, backless gown provided, then sit on the bed to feed Kayla but stand again to turn the gown around so she can access her brunch. I'm so thirsty.

A nurse comes in at 9:30 to insert an IV into my hand, but surgery isn't scheduled until 11:30. "Is there any way we could wait?" I gesture toward Kayla, using her. "What with me breastfeeding and all?" The nurse is understanding.

"I'll come back in an hour," she says and allows me a swallow of water to wash down pills that will offset nausea, a common side effect of anesthesia. I tilt my head back and hold the plastic cup upside down to get every drop.

"Now I'm feeling nervous," I tell Sam, who nods while changing Kayla's diaper. He is subdued. When Kayla squirms and fusses, Sam decides to take her for a walk while I try to concentrate on a television talk show. Instead, I find myself eavesdropping on an older couple behind the thin curtain dividing the room. The woman is obviously in pain, but she tries to keep her moans muffled. Apparently she has had surgery more than once. I feel sad for her and, at the same time, thankful that my condition is relatively minor. The nurse strides in and announces, "They're coming for you now. We're ahead of schedule." An hour-and-a-half early. I'm glad to get it over with, but want to see Sam and Kayla before they take me away.

Good timing. While I'm climbing onto the stretcher, they show up and escort me as I am wheeled to a line of beds in a wide hallway. When it's time to go, Sam gives me a thumbs-up signal then waves Kayla's arm as I call from the rolling cot: "Her baby rattle is in the diaper bag. Don't forget to wash it if she drops it on the floor." He humors me by not rolling his eyes.

The last thing I remember in the operating room is someone in scrubs asking me about my daughter, a good diversion tactic, and then waking up in a room with seven other beds. I don't remember losing consciousness and I am surprised at my immediate alertness. I always thought people came out of anesthesia muttering groggily, "Where am I?" Still, having no memory of the last ninety minutes is an uncomfortable feeling. I never even saw the doctor.

The next day I am supposed to take it easy, so I leave Kayla with my Dad and go to a movie, *The Secret Garden*. It's healing for me to see. I get to cry about my fears and release them during a dream sequence when Mary can't find her mother in the garden, and I feel elated as flowers bloom and young Master Colin learns how to walk.

In the days that follow, my thoughts turn back to life. My doctor calls and jokes that I was a bit out of it when he last spoke to me. He assures me he was there and it looks like he got all the dysplasia. He'll look at the cells again under a microscope in a couple of months. For now, he says, everything looks good.

Diapering Mom

Afton, Minnesota

"I just diapered my mom! Incredible! I didn't think I could ever do such a thing," I wrote on an eerily euphoric, sleepless winter morning, a week before my seventy-nine-year-old mother died.

I've diapered four brothers and my two children. But to diaper my stoic, Scandinavian mother? It seemed totally foreign and frightening to me to be a caretaker for a seriously ill adult, or more specifically, my self-reliant but terminally ill mother. Why did I fear it so?

Maybe the strong physical and emotional barrier was naturally constructed by this strong, beautiful, but extremely modest woman who rarely complained or spoke of her body, certainly never exposing it to me. She also had unusual fears of the sick and dying, maybe because as a youngster she had watched a beloved brother die of typhoid fever.

I, too, had become a fifty-year-old bag of fears regarding the sick and dying. While many curious people are drawn to a car accident, I run the other way. When I have the flu, I'm convinced it will turn into pneumonia.

In my fear and denial, death seemed easier to face than physically caring for an aging, ailing parent. I had been with Mom when she received the news that cancer had almost completely blocked her colon and was rapidly taking over her liver. I sat incredulously alert while, true to her no-nonsense realism, she queried the doctor as to what steps needed to be taken. Her distraught husband rushed from the room, unable to hear the details of his wife's death sentence.

Prophetically, over a year ago, Mom had purchased a burial plot and funeral package, even written her own simple obituary in an effort to keep her children from experiencing any additional pain at the time of her death. Now with a flurry, she tied up any additional loose ends, signing a living will, distributing personal mementos, instructing us to give her modest wardrobe to the needy.

She then immediately underwent surgery for the sole purpose of making her last months or weeks more comfortable. But after one painful week of recovery in the hospital, she spent only two peaceful days at home before a secondary infection, and a rapid loss of appetite and subsequent weight loss, left her with a weak body, a heavy heart, and a grieving family.

My father and I had been taking turns staying up to hear Mom when she needed help getting to the bathroom. Because of her extreme weakness, we feared her falling, breaking a hip, and adding further pain to her misery. But even with a baby monitor, my father did not always hear her, and so it was my second night without sleep. Caring for my mom was a roller-coaster ride of emotions. It was gut-wrenching to watch her rapid loss of self-sufficiency and the pain in her eyes.

As lightheartedly as possible in the middle of the night, I suggested adult diapers to her. She was visibly relieved at the possibility of a solution to her embarrassment.

The hospice nurse had left a bag of supplies the previous day and I remembered seeing what I thought were adult diapers. Even though my past diapering experiences had been performed with safety pins and cloth diapers, I had watched and occasionally helped younger mothers apply the modern-day disposable wonders. But these diapers had no adhesive tabs. And they were square.

After a tragicomic attempt with Scotch tape, I started to panic. Even though I had earlier in the day put a plastic sheet under her regular sheet, my Mom was inconsolable.

By this time, my father had joined the search for a solution, and with a tormented desire to help his wife, he cast aside his pride and privacy and revealed his own problems resulting from several prostate cancer surgeries by offering his "drip collectors." Although he did not call them that, he was naively unable to picture the ineffectiveness in Mom using the absorbent pouches that are anatomically designed for men. Inside I cried for him, but outwardly I reassured him that we would figure out a solution to Mom's discomfort. Then I remembered the twenty-four-hour phone number the hospice angels of mercy had left with us.

The Ask-A-Nurse on duty patiently explained without a trace of condescension that I was trying to use "Chucks," which are protective pads, not diapers. She suggested I try a twenty-four-hour grocery store. I blessed her in my heart. Nurses are supreme. They treat the sick and the dying and they know the simple answers to stupid questions we never dare ask a "busy" doctor.

My father worried about me driving alone at night in the sub-zero temperature, but was visibly relieved. I hurried out to my frigid car warmed by the excitement of removing one more hurdle in my Mom's last journey, a cheap fix for $15.

Back home, she called out, wondering why the front door was opening so late. She was thrilled with my successful mission. She quickly threw all caution and modesty to the wind, and with super human strength, lifted up her gaunt haunches and—presto—her first-ever string bikini!

"You've gone far beyond the call of duty," she said. "But what a load off my mind." In the morning the "disposable guards" were dry and we'd all had a peaceful sleep.

Mom momentarily reverted to her chronic mother-worry mode and admonished, "You could have been hurt going out alone in the middle of the night." I didn't mind. I was still basking in the glow. We had broken down a physical and emotional barrier. Besides, she still had the struggle of dying to attend to. Her passage was made just a little bit easier.

When she died a week later with most of her pride intact, I was humbled by the awesome gift she had given me. I felt like a kid again. I had diapered my Mom and she had made it easy. She helped me to face my own fears. She let me help her die.

Choosing to Rejoice

Holly Kofsky
Pottsdown, Pennsylvania

Naomi, you should have been perfect. You look perfect when I see you, when I hold you, when I touch you. I had many plans for us. I thought it would all come naturally. I would read you stories and you would laugh and snuggle up close to me. We could enjoy the museum together and talk about all that was before us. I looked forward to watching you gain independence as you went to school and made your own friends. I took it all for granted. I see that now.

Benjamin, you should have been born perfect. You look perfect when I see you, when I hold you, when I touch you. I thought you would enable me to experience what it was like to be the mother of a "normal" child. I envisioned you helping, and teaching, and protecting your sister. I thought you'd give me the opportunity to compare you with other babies and to inwardly boast of your milestones. You should have seen only one pediatrician rather than all those specialists. You should have allowed me to sit back and watch you blossom. Both of you should have allowed me to be one of the crowd. You shouldn't have isolated me. I thought you came to this world to join me, but instead I must join you.

Mom, this is Naomi. I am perfect. Do not mourn me. Mourn your image of me. I am not suffering, for this is all I know. This is what I do best. Being me. I cannot live up to your image of me. Recognize me for who I am. Respect me for who I am. Love me for who I am. I love you.

Mom, this is Benjamin. You can choose to be angry. You can choose to be sad. You can choose to deny who and what I am. You can choose to look inside.

You can choose to accept. You can choose to observe and discover. You can even choose to rejoice. I am not the cause of your pain. You are. You have chosen it with your beliefs and expectations of what should have been. Let it go and you will find me. I am special. I love you.

I Never Imagined

Cheryl Guenther
Webster, New York

I imagined motherhood like I imagined a vacation. I had visions of perfection, happiness, clear skies, and smooth sailing. I never envisioned difficulties. But, motherhood, like vacations, can turn out to be less than perfect—especially if your child is disabled.

As the mother of a disabled child, I went through all the stages that many losing a loved one go through. Denial, bargaining, blaming, anger, frustration, and finally, acceptance. It wasn't until I accepted this fate that I was able to take charge of the situation and begin working to maximize my child's potential.

The operative word, here, is *work*. I read everything I could about the disability; I sought out support groups, went to lectures and workshops, talked to doctors, and education professionals, and researched the recommended medicines. During the school years, I took on the difficult task of becoming my child's advocate, speaking up on behalf of his needs to insure that he wasn't shortchanged educationally or socially. Later on, I had to teach my son how to be his own advocate. I worked with my son to uncover whatever strengths and talents were there, so he didn't see himself solely in terms of his disability, but in terms of his ability. It was up to me to nurture and help him build on his strengths, as I discovered in our experience that his schools only focused on his disability. And, when the regular school placement didn't meet his needs, I began the search for one that would—and somehow found the money for it when the insurance didn't cover it.

Even with the feeling of well-being that taking positive steps brought, the struggle continued. Each gain, each inroad, was offset by failure, false starts, faltering steps. Just when I didn't think I could bear the pain of it all one more day, somehow, after a good night's sleep, I found the strength to persevere. As time went, on I become somewhat used to, and better at, doing what had to be done. Slowly, slowly, there were gains.

When my son achieved independence from me—not in the way I perceived at first, never that, but independence on his own terms, I had a surprising insight. I realized that, by being forced into a kind of motherhood that I would never have chosen, would have actively avoided, I learned some things that I never would have known without the experience.

I learned to be eminently more compassionate and understanding of others, disabled or not. I am slow to blame, for I have felt what unfortunates feel. I have learned how to survive a seemingly insurmountable obstacle—a useful life skill. I have experienced unreasonable pleasure in small steps well taken; I no longer need bells and whistles to bring me joy. When I encounter shallow people, I realize that I have a depth of knowledge and insight of which they have no concept, and probably never will.

What happened here? Could it be that this nightmare thrust upon me was actually a gift? Could it be that, in the end, I am even glad to have been through this experience, arduous as it was? I can only answer in the affirmative. Yes, it was tough; yes, there were dark days, months, years; yes, I kicked and screamed and railed the whole way, mostly inwardly. But, by picking myself up and carrying on day after day, success, though different than I envisioned, was finally, decisively achieved. And I am better because of all of it.

Asymmetry Has Its Own Kind Of Grace

Laurie Krug
Coconut Grove, Florida

Physically challenged, handicapped, disabled—these are all labels that might apply to my daughter, Kate. She was born with a rare, congenital syndrome called Klippel-Trenaunay. Her left leg is bigger than her right and her left foot was so deformed that it was not functional. Her foot was amputated when she was six months old. I used to perceive Kate in terms of her disability. In fact, when we first learned that Kate had a problem with her left leg, her disability was all that I could imagine of my yet unborn child.

Because I was forty when I was pregnant with my daughter, I was worried that Kate might be less than perfect. I was overjoyed when my amniocentesis results were normal. I thought we were home free. Weeks later, during an ultrasound, I noticed that the technician spent an unusual amount of time looking at the screen. She left abruptly, telling my husband and me that she was going to get the doctor. I knew then that something was wrong. Terror struck my heart and I began crying before we even spoke to the doctor. All he could tell us was that Kate's left foot was extremely deformed and that her entire left leg was enlarged. I remember thinking, "Why? Why our child? Why us?"

I cannot describe the excruciating heartbreak my husband and I felt. I could not cry enough, or scream enough to exorcise my disappointment and sorrow. Our dreams of a perfect little girl were replaced with fear. We didn't know if Kate would ever be able to walk, or ride a tricycle, or greet her Dad when he came home from work. I was terrified that she might have other disabilities that ultrasound couldn't detect. Most of all, I was afraid that I wouldn't be able to love her because she wasn't perfect.

The rest of my pregnancy was a dizzying dance with geneticists, who tried to diagnose Kate in utero; ultrasonographers, who tracked the growth of Kate's leg; neonatologists, who prepared for her birth; and endocrinologists, who kept my maternal diabetes in line. None of these specialists could tell us how impaired Kate would be.

Kate was born by planned C-section and spent her first seven days in a neonatal intensive-care unit hooked up to a heart monitor. I was overwhelmed with her care when we brought her home. The neonatologists said she might go into heart failure. The pediatrician said she could get an infection in her leg. The plastic surgeon said he could not fix her foot and the orthopedist recommended amputation.

Those first few months, everyone, including me, focused on Kate's disability. Her leg was the first thing most people noticed. It was not a pretty sight. Her plastic surgeon was speechless upon seeing her leg. I was concerned about taking her out of the house. I didn't know how I would ever handle the inevitable comments and questions. I didn't know what I would say.

Eventually, I did go out with Kate. I learned how to ignore people's stares. On my bad days, I'd just stare right back at them with fire in my eyes. I learned when to answer questions and when to pretend I was deaf. I learned that some people are incredibly insensitive. I also discovered how compassionate and caring most people are. The most important thing I learned was to love Kate.

I began focusing on what Kate could do instead of what she couldn't do. In essence, I began noticing the rest of Kate. Kate had the endearing habit of stroking my arm while she breast-fed—up, down, up—in three-quarter time. When she was three months old she looked directly into my eyes and grinned at me. I loved rocking her to sleep at night. She is the only human being I've ever known who is actually comforted by my singing voice.

Kate was hospitalized five times before her first birthday. She has had three major surgeries and two life-threatening infections. Through all of this, Kate has been amazingly resilient. She learned to crawl despite the extra weight of her left

leg. She stood and cruised using the coffee table for support at ten months old. When she got her prosthesis, she was walking within a month. Despite all the trauma she has been through in her short life, she is fairly well-adjusted. The only lasting emotional reminder is her understandable fear of anyone who sports a white lab coat.

Kate just turned two. She still isn't perfect. She won't share, pitches temper tantrums in public places, eats spaghetti with her hands, and never sleeps. She teases the cats and dog, insists on wearing her dress shoes to the muddy playground, and continually escapes from her car seat. She is a typical two-year-old who happens to have a prosthesis where her left foot should be.

I don't see Kate as being imperfect now. What I do is see a courageous, spunky, beautiful little girl who taught her old Mom a few things about life. I've learned that Katie is not her disability. She is the sum of all her parts. I know now what I couldn't have known while I was pregnant—that asymmetry has its own kind of grace. I need not have worried about my ability to love Kate, for I love her without measure.

# Waiting

Gloria Watson
Bloomington, Minnesota

While waiting for your sentence at home, I am comforted by pacing among familiar objects. A brain scan was needed. You are my firstborn. Our brown eyes speak that truth. I try to picture an ugly mass growing inside of that chestnut-brown head of hair. I want to believe nothing so foul could grow inside you, my innocent child.

You, who have taught me so much about love and living, now teach me about fear and dying.

What I wait for today is beyond me. It is one of those faith things. Floating between dark and light, not knowing if or even when it will land. Have I believed enough? Is my faith strong enough for all of us? You and your Dad always tagging along at my spiritual heels just for the ride, I'm hoping this ride comes free.

$\mathcal{U}$pside Down

Paula Pellegrino
Rochester, New York

My oldest child, Katie, turned three on a typically pleasant spring day. My son, Joey, was twenty-two months old, and my third child, Gina, was due to be born in a matter of weeks. My parents were in town to celebrate with us, and all was well, or so I thought. Katie had been feeling and looking rather tired, not quite herself for the past few days. As there was already an annual physical scheduled with our pediatrician the following week, and her puffy eyes, slight sniffle, and no fever led me to suspect allergies, I felt no immediate need to hurry her in to see the doctor.

By the next day, I had changed my mind very quickly. Katie hit her cheek on a chair and something about the bruise alerted me. I had never seen anything like that deep purple mark, and even to my untrained eyes, it was anything but normal.

Even though I told myself not to panic, I did a day later when, beneath her skin, I noticed tiny, multiple bruises that I later learned were called "petechia." I immediately called our doctor and was told to come into the office that morning. From there, we were sent to the hospital for tests, and by then I was sure that something was terribly wrong. Within a couple of hours, my husband and I were told that in all likelihood Katie had leukemia, and the next day that diagnosis was confirmed. Katie's initial stay in the hospital lasted six weeks, which, needless to say, turned our world upside down.

Exactly two weeks after that horrible day, I gave birth to a healthy baby girl, Gina. Within a matter of days, I went from experiencing the paralyzing fear of possibly losing one of my precious children to the amazing joy of

 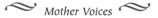

giving life to our newest one. It was probably the most bittersweet moment of my life.

My son, Joe, still just a baby himself at the time, had the least immediate needs and received so much love and care from everyone else that I didn't spend much time with him. I feel as though I had abandoned him, even now. Fortunately, we have a wonderful family, and they were all there for us to do whatever had to be done. My mother stayed with us that entire summer, and in truth, saved us all. She became Gina's surrogate mother, Joey's playmate, and my soulmate. She is the one on whom I base my model of motherhood.

Our very courageous Kate received treatment for two years, but has been in remission for quite a while and is a very active second-grader. Joe is entering first grade this year, and can still change my mood from sunshine to rain, and back again in the blink of an eye. And sweet Gina, the little baby girl with whom I felt I never had enough time to bond, is now a preschooler who loves to sing and cuddle.

I sometimes think I haven't spent enough time with my kids, one on one, or altogether. I find myself observing other mothers with their children and wonder why they're never arguing or why they don't appear irritable or frazzled, as I so often am. Are they more patient, less selfish, more in tune with their kids?

This journey has left me in a constant state of uncertainty. Sometimes I feel as though I'm doing a pretty good job of mothering, but more often I am sure I'm blowing the whole thing.

The only thing I know for certain is that I love my children unconditionally, and upon that rock they build their foundation.

Smudges

Stephanie Szmyd
Davis, California

A life here, then gone. Leaving traces behind of clothes, toys, a toothbrush. Just possessions, nothing more. But what of the spirit? Activity? Life? Crayon marks on walls and...the handprint.

My friend had been meaning to clean that day. Angry at herself for being behind with her chores. Has it really been two years since she came to know a pain so unfathomable, so all-consuming that every element in her being changed?

"Hi, Mommie!" She still hears the voice. And the handprint. She's there! Isn't she?

And then, today, the cleaning company her husband insisted on hiring to help her "keep up," washed the windows. She dropped the groceries and ran to the place...gone, not even a streak. How could they? She collapsed, falling to her knees realizing the good-byes were never going to end.

In the same neighborhood, just two blocks away, a mother yells: "Kirsten! Stay away from that window! I just washed it!"

When does mothering end?

Nourishment

Nancy Veronen
Minneapolis, Minnesota

With love I gave you my breast, which you fed from hungrily, noisily, greedily.

With joy I gave you my heart, which again you doubled or tripled in size. Little babe, you invaded not only my body, but every aspect of my being.

I nourished you with a tranquillity I did not know I possessed. Tending to you, I tended to me. Feeding you was feeding me. Loving you brought love to me.

Then you died, and my breasts were aching for Erica. Swollen with milk and no baby to feed. My heart so large with love, shattered inside, went on beating in a strange, irregular way. BEATING, beating, beating, BEATING. Pounding me with each heartbeat, forcing me to live without my child.

Many days I've often wondered who was feeding whom?

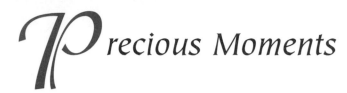

Precious Moments

Lauri-Ann Farmer
Sarina, Ontario, Canada

After five years of trying to conceive a child, my husband, Michael, and I learned that I was pregnant with twins as a result of in-vitro fertilization. We were ecstatic with happiness until twenty-five weeks into the pregnancy when I went into premature labor and gave birth to Jesse William and Ryann Samantha, 1 lb., 11 oz. and 1 lb. 8 oz., respectively.

"Fifty-fifty chance;" "maybe;" "no guarantees;" "handicapped;" "relax;" "I'm sorry;" "I love you;" "Congratulations;" "It's a boy;" "It's a girl."

"Are they alive? Oh, God, please save my babies." I studied the faces of the doctors and nurses, willing them to give me hope, too terrified to ask for it. But the memories that are the clearest are of our moms...who, without words, told me that they would have given their lives for this not to be happening to us. I realized in those moments that this is what being a mom is all about. Loving your children so much that you are willing to take all their pain. I was tested on this lesson much sooner than I could have expected.

One week after their birth and still on life support, I was able to hold Ryann for thirty glorious seconds! I cried so hard my nose bled. A few days later, I held Jesse for the briefest amount of time and I promised him I would bring him and his sister home. One week later, Jesse turned gray and the doctors told us he might not make it through the night. Sitting in the "crisis" room with the medical staff, my defenses kicked in again, and my memories are of the vast array of shoes the staff was wearing. Two weeks later, Jesse had gone from bad to worse. I prayed that God would take me and not my son; I bartered, trying to find a suitable trade-off.

I begged for a "sign." I made promises too numerous to remember. I was terrified to have a negative thought for fear that this would be interpreted as giving up and I talked endlessly to Jesse hoping my voice would somehow renew his body. I was afraid to be critical of anyone, thinking that my actions may be used against me, and Jesse would be taken as punishment for my unkind thoughts or actions.

Without saying a word to each other, Michael and I decided that we needed to put Jesse's life ahead of our own and allow him the freedom to decide his fate. I knew that I was hanging on to Jesse because I didn't know how I would survive without him.

One month after his incredible birth, Jesse William died in my arms. I cherish this day because I was finally able to see my son without tubes, tape, and frowns. His wee body was free of all invasions and he was cozy and warm in a blanket made by Grandma. My eyes had never seen such a peaceful sight as I stared at him, afraid to blink, attempting to burn his image and spirit in my mind so that I would never forget the sight of his nose, mouth, or toes. This day was my last shot at being a real mom to him, of establishing memories of us together that would allow me to share his life with his twin sister and give me the strength to face each day. I played with my baby. I sang lullabies, read storybooks, bathed, dressed, cuddled, rocked, and gave him Eskimo kisses. I was bursting with pride of my son, of his spirit and courage.

On their expected due date, three-and-one-half months after their birth, I brought my babies home. Ryann Samantha is now two-and-a-half years old, healthy and happy, and Jesse's ashes are kept in our bedroom. Jesse continues to send me "signs" of his love, and a little over a year later, McKenna Rae was born.

I have been blessed and humbled by this experience. I cherish and celebrate each step, smile, diaper, tantrum, and cuddle with Ryann and McKenna. They are an endless hunger for me and I look at them each day as if I am seeing them for the first time, hoping they will never see the desperation in my eyes as I try to hang onto each moment.

_As_ Time

Goes By

The Pink is Out

Colleen Carroll Gordon and
Deborah Gordon Cooper
Hopkins and Duluth, Minnesota

A Mother's Memory...

Each family has a litany, a loving, lilting liturgy to hold them close, to keep them strong, to buoy them up against life's storms, their magic keys.

Excitement dots all history: "The British are coming," "A man's on the moon," "The pink is out!"

This is no pink sunset to be taken lightly. A pink sky is to embolden and enliven, to lift one's spirits and give heart to the weary...

A little girl hangs upside-down on her jungle gym. The magical pink is everywhere. It is almost more than she can bear! She calls us all. We join the shout.

"The pink is out. The pink is out!"

This is a wild and wanton pink to wallow in, to drink in, to sink in. It covers you, envelops you; it is a beauty to savor your whole life.

The pink came out on her wedding day. It transformed the freeway into ribbon bouquets, shivering and shimmering, showering stars.

We each have our vistas of setting suns that serenade us when our day is over. What food for the soul, what memories. Pinks you ache to taste and touch—seeing never seems quite sufficient.

I doubt I will ever again see a pink that gave such clarity to blackened, leaf-stripped forest trees as we paddled home late one summer evening. Or how the sun dappled St. Martin's dome in the French town of Tours, or peach-puffed clouds as our plane went airborne.

What a wondrous gift for a family. A little girl with her kaleidoscope who knew the monumental clout of being there when the pink is out.

A Daughter's Reply...

When I was three and playing in the yard one evening, pleading for five more minutes then five more again, then running and stumbling, beating at the door with small, sticky fists and clamoring, "Come and see! The pink is out! The pink is out!" you'd always come flying, wiping your hands on your apron with all of the lights shining in your face, too, to look with me as if you'd never before seen the evening sky bloom open like a rose, its quiet ecstasy unfolding in us, too.

"Holy, holy, holy!"

You, who taught me everything that matters in this life—the music and the magic in the sky and looking all the way into the eyes of one another. We know by heart the colors at the close of the day, the tender radiant endings that open just before dark.

$\mathcal{N}$early Two

Killeen Pilon
Seattle, Washington

Your heart beats without doubt and your dark eyes are often wide with wonder. They brim with happiness at the sight of a dog on the street in spite of the fact that the neighbor's dog nearly bit your face. Your mother screamed and struck the dog while you said, "No doggie, no," having learned one of life's hard lessons.

Your eyes dance with excitement at the sound of fire trucks responding to human carelessness and possible tragedy, things you do not know about yet. Hazel in color, they dart nervously from pony to pony when we visit the park. You want to pet a dappled one, not ride her, even though she's tethered to a spoke of the big iron wheel that assures she can walk only so fast and in circles.

We ride the small train, which passes near the horses through the park. Your diaper is dirty, but your zest for this new adventure transcends your discomfort as if you were a Zen master (which you may well be).

A veil clouds those bright eyes when your fever climbs to 105 degrees and you vomit for two days straight and we fear the worst. The flatness of your hazel eyes brings tears to my own, and I wish I could take on the sickness for you.

When you are well again, we snort like pigs and meow like cats and bark like dogs and walk through the house on our hands and knees. You howl with a laughter that infects me with a kind of pure joy that I haven't felt in years.

We quietly wait for our dinner at the Mexican take-out down the street. Your face and hands are grimy from helping me repot the porch plants. Your arms entwine my leg and the señora smiles when she hands us our food.

When I take you in my arms that night, to tuck you in your crib, I am holding you and another child as well. Feather light, I hold the memory of your mother, when she was not quite two.

Revelations in the Rain

Lorraine White
Newton, Iowa

The warm rain falls, orchestrated by gentle June breezes. What a miraculous gift we experience as we walk hand-in-hand. The rain tenderly envelops us.

"Mama," he chatters. A three-year-old approaching thirty. "God gives us the rain, uh, so the trees and the leaves can grow…and I like the sound of the wheels on my Hot Wheels when I go fast through the water." His final words emerge in a rush.

I visualize her through a misty haze. Feelings of warmth and well-being caress me. Her hair is as white as new fallen snow. Her heart-shaped face is weathered and brown; it feels comforting to my touch. "This is million-dollar rain," she whispers to the child in me. I remember, Grandma. I remember well.

A poignantly clear vision beckons. His skin is incredibly smooth and sweet-smelling. He nuzzles my breast impatiently, demanding nourishment. My husband watches his son and me in wonder.

Remembrances of my mother arise. With graceful serenity she sets aside her apron and battered baking pans. I retrieve them instinctively. She takes my son in her arms and fills his head with tales of the seasons of her youth.

Now, the day beckons, filled with endless tasks and boundless possibilities. As the rain continues to fall I realize with startling clarity how blessed I am.

Coming Home

Marion Franck
Davis, California

I just took my thirteen-year-old daughter on her first trip to Europe. The weather was sunny, the daffodils in bloom. We stayed with friends. One couple in London and another in Paris, and while they trudged off to their everyday jobs, Beth and I slept late under feather comforters. Then we breakfasted on English jam or French croissants, thumbed through guidebooks, and let whim propel us from one place to another like a gentle wind. After the Eiffel Tower, how about a boat ride on the Seine?

In the evenings, we reunited with our friends, dined (often in restaurants) and talked about their countries and our respective lives. I became so sated with good company, mild weather, and abundant food and wine, that I felt as full and soft as a boulangerie cream puff.

Re-entry is not going well.

To acquaintances, I explain I'm jet-lagged, and it's true as I collapse into bed before nine-thirty and awaken wide-eyed and sleep-deprived at five in the morning. I am unenthusiastic about my supper at six and ravenous at ten (dinnertime in Paris).

More to the point, I don't want to cook that supper, nor the lunch and breakfast that precede it. Nor do I want to do laundry, change the guinea pig cages, exercise, or collect for charities.

I want to be served.

I want to sit at a small round table in a Parisian café, as I did only three weeks ago, and say to the waiter who wipes the table with a white cloth from his back pocket, "S'il vous plait, un café."

I don't want to get into my hulky, practical van and shuttle to the supermarket for sandwich meat.

I stall in front of the dishwasher, and even a finished load, whose sparkle used to please me, only means I have to put the dishes away.

I want to go back to work, but when I get there I seem to have forgotten the job. What was I supposed to do next? And what effect was it supposed to have, anyway?

When I'm not newly returned from vacation, I'm happy at home. There are clothes to clean and sandwiches to make, but the sameness of the days makes the differences between them more striking. On a calm lake the slightest stone causes a ripple. And I love the little distractions in my life: lunch with a friend, a good television show, a sentence I wrote well.

Maybe the problem is that people don't take long vacations anymore. When I was young, my father earned two weeks a year, later three, and we took them at a stretch. The vacations always seemed long to me; I couldn't wait to snuggle under my own covers, catch up on magazines, telephone my friends. Even the year we went to Italy, I was thrilled to get home. English was a warm nest and I felt wonder in an American supermarket. After a second European sojourn in my twenties—five blissful months of college in France—the supermarket did not entrance, but my own bed still felt wonderful.

When my daughter and I pulled into Paris on our Chunnel train after careening through the countryside at 186 miles per hour, tears formed in my eyes like dew on a lawn.

Twenty-five years ago I was young in Paris, and I learned to blow smoke rings, to drink coffee in tiny cups, and to speak French. Men followed me. This time it was the street artists—male and female—who pursued me, whispering loudly, "Please, madame, this is your daughter? Very beautiful. May I draw her?"

Bright with excitement, Beth did look lovely, and I felt a twinge of envy for the life that still awaits her.

Her charcoal portrait, still curled at the edges, is pressed under books in our living room. I pause next to it as I roam the house in the early morning darkness, restless, unaccountably sad. Our trip was too short I tell myself, or something was.

I stand in my daughter's doorway. She's sound asleep, hugging her pillow, growing so fast.

The Wooden Bowl

Abbie Katz
Newton, Pennsylvania

When my sons were born, I asked myself, "Who will inherit the wooden bowl now?" It was the wooden bowl so lovingly and patiently used by my grandmother to teach me how to cook. Her legacy lived in that bowl, a simple implement now nearly sixty years old. The bowl was once round, but with all of the chopping and turning, its edges have been carved out to a more oval-looking shape. She taught me to prepare chopped meat in that bowl and from that simple act of cooking in that wooden bowl came my profound love for her, my family, and my passion for cooking.

Ah, the wooden bowl—it is one of the few precious things I have from my grandmother and the house I grew up in as a child. It is perhaps more alive than the other inanimate objects I have from that idealized time of my life. She and I used it together. Nanny rewarded me for my help by letting me taste the mixed chopped meat. I rendered many an opinion as to whether more salt or pepper was needed in the mixture. Of all of the wonderful meals I can produce, my chopped meat dishes are still favorites of friends and family.

Actually, my grandmother was a terrible cook, with not one ounce of culinary creativity. But because she let me participate with her, my interest in cooking began at the ripe old age of five.

So, now that I have two sons, I wonder what type of legacy I will pass on to them? Will they, too, look at this wooden bowl with the same affection and sentimental view? My almost three-and-a-half-year-old, Philip, chops with me in the bowl now. He already knows about refining ground meat and that chopping

must be done in the opposite direction of the grain—a great way to teach kids about horizontal and vertical directions. I lovingly guide his undeveloped hand motion, while we chop or mix things in the wooden bowl. The best result of all of this is that he wants to know more about my grandmother and the things I did with her. I suspect that when my pudgy twenty-two-month-old son, Andrew, is old enough, we'll all be using that wooden bowl with as much love as any legacy can provide.

Gingerbread Men

Paula Elsloo
Wayland, New York

Any sensible mother would have bought graham crackers. After all, it was only a preschool birthday party. But as it drew closer I became sentimental and tender and made rash promises. I believe the phrase "anything you want" might have been used.

After much thought, my daughter settled on gingerbread men as the perfect treat. She wanted to make them from scratch. She also decided that each tiny face should be decorated with a different expression. She wanted a parade of happy, sad, angry, and surprised ginger people.

There are sixteen kids, a teacher and an aide, in Anna's class and I could read the icing on the wall. Mixing, rolling, cutting, baking, and painting faces was going to hold her attention for about ten minutes. The rest of the equation seemed painfully obvious. Someone much older than four was going to get stuck making an awful lot of cookies.

Willingly, almost eagerly, I took my place in a long line of mothers with something to prove.

When I wasn't much older than Anna, my own mother let me choose my birthday cake from a cookbook full of improbably arranged and tinted food. My choice was an elaborate castle with pink frosting walls, candy cane pillars, and windows framed in red licorice. It was the most beautiful cake in the world. It was also impossibly intricate. Frank Lloyd Wright couldn't have built this damned thing with its turrets and towers, drawbridges and moats.

I don't remember the bakery cake we surely ended up with that year. But here's the strange part. When my mother died, that castle was the first image that came

back to me. Out of a lifetime together, that is what surfaced and spent the night as I numbly scrambled to make airline reservations and pack a suitcase to go to my mother's funeral.

Sometimes I picture her, the woman from whom I inherited my impatience, swearing quietly to herself as she struggled to glue sponge cake walls together with frosting. My mother, a crazed perfectionist, would be horrified that this vision is what I retain and cherish over all her carefully orchestrated successes.

The day that Anna wanted her gingerbread men fell in the middle of a busy week. I really didn't have time for an evening-long baking project. I said yes anyway, kicking myself for it, knowing it wasn't for Anna and her shining, hopeful face. Instead, it was an offering to a mother I seldom got along with, in remembrance of a cake we never ate.

Anna only heard the yes.

The Gift

Stephanie Szmyd
Davis, California

When I went back East to visit my sister this summer, she gave me a small, brown journal. Inside was the inscription, "To help capture thoughts over future cups of coffee." On the front was one word, "Writer." She had found the perfect way to acknowledge my aspirations.

Oh, the joys of the perfect gift! It screams out from the giver, "I know." We all try so hard to get others to see ourselves as we do. That age-old teen lament, "You just don't understand!" can be just as true for a forty-one-year-old wife and mother in the suburbs. When the necessity of the job requires endless hours of scrubbing toilets, making beds, mowing lawns, then rushing over to the school to help out in the classroom, little time is left for the poet buried deep inside.

In childhood, it was almost magical the way someone always seemed to know exactly what we wanted. Of course, the pony may never have made it to the front yard, but there was the bride doll, the roller skates, the new bike. There was usually one gift that said, "I know who you are and you are loved very much."

My own daughters are getting to the age now where they are questioning the mechanism of all this.

"I can't wait till I'm grown-up. Then I'll know if Santa is real and who the Easter Bunny is," my youngest announces one afternoon as we're stopped at a red light on our way to her piano lesson.

A smile comes to my lips that I hope she doesn't see and I think to myself, "Trust me, you don't want to know."

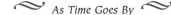

The sad truth is that right around the time children start asking how the magic works they begin hiding their feelings and dreams behind closed bedroom doors and monosyllabic answers to the question, "How was school today?" Little do they know that they're closing out the one person who really does know who Santa and the Easter Bunny are.

Sometimes I think we spend the rest of our lives trying to open our own doors. Like someone lost in the woods, we try to retrace our steps back to another time. Whatever happened, we ask, to that child who could so effortlessly say, "This is what I want. This is what I need." Unfortunately, most of us are so good at closing doors and evading questions that others don't bother anymore to find out how our day was or what is really behind the sullen silence.

Over the years, I've made peace with the fact that my own childhood days are over. And the trade-offs are fine. I cherish my emotional independence and the freedom of being able to move about without my inner-self so readily visible. And, if that means getting a bread-maker instead of the book I really wanted, so be it. But every once in a while, as I wedge my foot in the way of three little bedroom doors getting ready to shut, I wish my own heart was on my sleeve just a tad. Sometimes moms want bride dolls, too.

Chanukah

Sandra B. Tulchinsky
Mendota Heights, Minnesota

We lived in the old house then. The linen closet was in the big bedroom, the one with lavender walls where my parents slept.

Every year, Sammy and I would sneak into the big bedroom, open the door to the linen closet and carefully search among the sheets and towels for our Chanukah presents. That's where my mother always hid them. The presents were wrapped, of course, but Sammy and I would shake each parcel and offer opinions and counsel on its contents.

This year, however, the linen closet was empty, save sheets and towels. No presents. Sammy and I looked everywhere. We even shook out the linens to make sure that our mother had not become devious and really hidden them. But still, no presents.

"Not fair," pronounced Sammy.

"Do you think they forgot?" I asked, worried that I would never get the doll that I longed to have and said was the only thing that I wanted.

"Naw," said Sammy, seeming not the least bit concerned. He was twelve, six years my senior and knew everything important.

It was harder than usual to wait for Chanukah to begin. We received one present each evening—after we lit the candles on our menorah. Our presents consisted of seven little knickknacks, and one good present, something special. We never figured them all out, but after our annual exploration of the linen closet, Sammy and I usually could guess some of the presents. But this year, for the first time, we didn't know what we were getting.

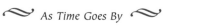

As the youngest, I got to select my present first. I went for the biggest box. I tore off the wrapper and inside, there she was—the doll that I wanted. She had long, wavy black hair like mine and I loved her immediately. I promptly named her Harriet, after my favorite cousin.

Sammy chose next. He, too, selected the biggest of his presents. I could tell by the shape of the box, a shallow rectangle, that it was some kind of board game. Tearing off the wrapping paper confirmed it. Sammy looked at the bright red and yellow box, then at my mother as his eyes welled and a big tear fell down his cheek. He didn't say a word. He carefully placed the game down on the floor, turned and walked out of the room. It was very quiet for a moment; then, the sound of Sammy slamming his bedroom door filled the whole house.

My mother looked hurt. She followed Sammy upstairs to his room while my father suggested that I go to my own room to play with my new doll.

The door to Sammy's room was open and I overheard part of the conversation as I sat on my bed, stroking Harriet's black hair. Sammy was disappointed, betrayed. This game was for little kids, for babies. How could they ever think that it was a good Chanukah gift for him?

He was crying and Sammy rarely cried. The last time I remembered him crying was when he got hit in the eye with a baseball and had to get stitches. I'd never known Sammy to be so upset.

I could hear my mother's voice. She spoke softly, slowly. She talked about how sorry she was that Sammy didn't like his present. She talked about how the act of giving was more important than the gift itself and at twelve, Sammy was old enough to understand that. She spoke about how it had been a hard year and a struggle to buy those gifts and how she wished there was enough to go out and buy him something new. She talked about how much she loved him and didn't mean to hurt his feelings.

Sammy would have none of it. My mother sighed, said that she was sorry and left him. Sammy cried himself to sleep.

I was so angry with her. How could she do that? She should have known better than to pick out a game for babies. She should have gotten him something good, something special. And to leave him there crying. That's not how you're supposed to feel on Chanukah...

Mindy is seven now. I await Chanukah with great excitement, delighting in the smile that lights up her face as the wrapping paper comes flying off the presents.

We follow my family's tradition and Mindy gets one present for each night of the festival, right after we light our menorah. She gets seven knickknacks and one present that's special. I try to hide the wrapped presents where she can find them.

I'm sure she's guessed what's in some of the boxes but she always saves the biggest box for the last night.

"This is my special one, isn't it?" she asks, already working on the wrapping paper before I can answer. My husband winks at me and I smile back. Then I look at Mindy, all smiles and dimples, as the paper comes flying off. A Power Ranger Action Doll. I visited several stores before I found the green one, her favorite. Mindy stares at the box for a moment and then bursts into tears.

"Honey, what's wrong? It's the green one, your favorite," I begin.

"Power Rangers and dolls are for babies, not second-graders," she wails. "I wanted a magic set—the big one! You promised!"

I was sure she'd be thrilled with a Power Ranger doll—especially the green one. "Honey, you love the Power Rangers," I plead. "And Mommy thought that's what you wanted for Chanukah."

Tears stream down Mindy's face. I feel terrible. She says nothing, staring at the box, and that makes me feel even worse. I say something about how bad Daddy and I feel about selecting the wrong gift; about how the act of giving is more important than the gift and that she's a big girl now and should understand; about how tight things are since her Daddy was laid off and my hours were cut back and how I wish there was enough money to go out right now and buy the magic set.

"You're so mean!" she sobs.

Yes, I think. I am. Just like my mother.

Gardening On

Susan Guralnick
Seattle, Washington

I remember my mother on her knees carefully weeding, lovingly cutting blooms, watering and feeding her sweet young plants, nurturing them along. I remember my grandmother planting her yellow coreopsis in the tiniest square of dirt outside her apartment door, and black-eyed Susans named for me to welcome us in.

I cannot believe I am doing this now. Standing in my own garden with surprise and delight. I work here in little bursts of love and energy drinking in shapes and colors. My garden brings me simple joy.

I still know in my heart that my mother sneaks here in the dark to nurture my flowers. I do not know the things I should. I just took that chance to grow. As the cry "Mom" floats across the yard I look around. Is it my brother calling for her? I scratch my graying hair and see my son bounding over to show me a ladybug. I laugh, enjoying myself and my confusion.

Yes, my mother and grandmother hide in the foxglove bells, winking warmly at me from their pale yellow cocoons, smiling at the sight of my young son in the midst of it all.

A Graceful Flight

Dona McGovern
St. Cloud, Florida

In a cycle that continues like the seasons, I press a pie crust into an oversized pan that will not survive another generation. Nana once promised to fill the pie pan with New England huckleberries. Each summer in our suburban home she loaded it with green apples or hand-pitted cherries and decorated the crust. Her tiny hands massaged dough as well as my curiosity in the search of an improbable fruit known only to grandmothers. Returning to her home each summer I would perch on the horsehair seat of a black sedan and search among the pine scrub for the magic berries. "Next year we'll pick a bushel of huckleberries," she said, "and if you don't eat the lot I'll make you a pie that will make your tongue sing hymns and your belly roar like a lion for more."

Her Irish tongue was filled with lullabies and early morning "aaammmenns" soft as birdsong. She flitted about the kitchen between her good morning and good night pecks. I have no recollection of her ever being in any other room with the exception of the time I caught her undressing in the bathroom. I was young enough to believe elderly bodies were as fluid as the toga-clad saints and cherubs of church statues. The concept of pubic hair made as much sense as the atom bomb drills that interrupted recess. Backing out the door I closed my eyes and made the sign of the cross.

For days I stood by her side looking for signs of deterioration. There were her thick yellow fingernails and false teeth that she popped on and off her gums as she stood over the gas burners of our stove stirring oatmeal. Through her apron, cotton dress, and bra, I envisioned cow udders that had nursed my mother and aunts. Frightened and fascinated I finally asked, "Will my boobs look like yours?"

Her neck bobbed like a whooping crane as she coughed and twittered. Sometimes I see her face in my own as I look in the mirror at pursed lips and the tight bun I wrap around the crown of my head. The same shaking of her head from side to side as she put her tiny hand on my shoulder and said, "Only if you're lucky enough to live this long."

Genes willing, I fly into the face of old age with the promise of her huckleberry pie waiting for me in heaven. Much the way my daughters fly about the kitchen on holidays with my own mother, their Nana. All of us sail forward on wings that are lifted by laughter light as the crust on a huckleberry pie.

Crazy Quilt

Lee Brezina
Neehah, Wisconsin

The quilt lay folded in the chest. We always called it her hope chest. It was fragrant with the smell of cedar, as fresh as a piney forest, its path strewn with needles and footprints. As I turn the quilt top over, each piece stitched in its crazy pattern speaks to me of Mother.

Blue-checked gingham from the oversized apron, her kitchen uniform. Navy blue with shiny squiggles, her church and meeting dress. The feather stitching in yellow, blue, green, purple; was it artistic or the use of thread on hand?

The backing is a sugar sack dated 1931; that year a son was born, a husband gone. I find blue plaid flannel and a misshapen piece of an overall. As I touch each square, oblong, triangle, some fabrics coarse as gunny sacks, others smooth as cream, I see her at night by lamplight cutting, piecing and stitching sanity into her crazy quilt.

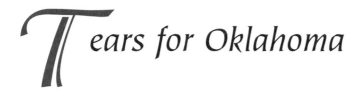

Tears for Oklahoma

Dawn M. Gorman
East Lansing, Michigan

I watched the television in horror. Broken bodies being carried from the rubble. Rag doll figures without names. Children of the harvest land. Lives taken without cause, without warning, bloodied babies, their eyes wide with terror, those still alive.

Mothers screaming outside trying to get in, trying to find their children. Children alone, buried, frightened, lying in the dusty dark. Reporters telling of the dead, using words like "sex undetectable," "burned beyond recognition," "decapitated."

I sit in the safety of my own home, on my living room floor with the sun shining on my back. In the safety of my home? You come and stand before me, a twinkling in your eyes and you snap your pudgy fingers and do a little dance as you tell a tale of Easter bunnies and baskets full of "yittle" eggs. You are breathless with excitement. Laughter rolls from me, then abruptly turns to tears and gasps and sobs, and I cry and cry.

The Frame is Frozen

Evelyn Thompson
Cleveland, Tennessee

I had gone to bed and was settling in to watch television when the phone rang. It was my twenty-one-year-old son's voice at the other end. All he said was "Mom" and I knew by his tone that something was very wrong.

"What's wrong, Mark?" I asked.

"Mom, it's my roommate, Slim, he's been in a terrible accident. I'm at the hospital and the doctor has told me he may not make it."

Slim was my son's roommate. They had attended college together. Mark explained to me that Slim had gone for a ride on the motorcycle he had just bought two days before. A teenage boy ran a stop sign. Slim hit him broadside.

"Mom, I just want you to pray for Slim," Mark said.

"Son, I will pray for him like he were you," I promised. And I did. But as the doctor had predicted, Slim did not make it.

My son called twice the next day. I wanted so much to be there to put my arms around him and comfort him. He was hurting so much. He was doing everything he could for the family. He had cleaned Slim's room and put everything in order. "Slim always left his room in a mess," he told me, sounding like a brother who had loved and accepted his friend just the way he was.

On Friday morning, the day before the funeral, I set out to find the little West Virginia town where Slim's funeral and my son would be. After driving six hours, I came to an interstate exit I knew would lead me to Hurricane, West Virginia. I stopped at the first service station I saw and asked for directions to the funeral home. I drove on, watching for my destination "off the road, to the right."

Sure enough, about five miles down the road, I looked to my right and there stood my son. My wonderful son, my handsome son, my cherished son, my living son.

For the next day and a half, I watched him be a man—strong and caring, comforting friends, talking to Slim's parents, introducing me to everyone he knew there, and carrying his friend's body to its last resting place. I watched as he stood beside the coffin staring, long after the funeral director thanked him and told him it was all over. I stood and waited.

I knew from the moment this whole tragedy began that there would come a time when he would be ready to talk. I drove and he talked. When he had said all he wanted and needed to say, I talked. I told him how my heart was so full of mixed emotions. While my heart was aching for Slim's family, I felt so fortunate that it wasn't him on that motorcycle. He understood what I was trying to say to him.

The minister at the funeral said, "Sometimes in our lives, the film that always seems to be rapidly moving through our camera stops and the frame is momentarily frozen. At these times, we stop and see where we have been and where we are going. This is one of those times." How true that statement was. My son and I had stopped that day and looked at our relationship. We were closer than we had been since the days I could pick him up and carry him. I knew the love between us had grown stronger and neither of us would ever be the same.

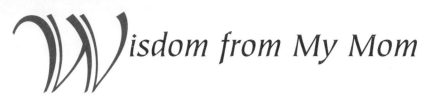isdom from My Mom

Gloria Watson
Bloomington, Minnesota

During the last fifteen years of my first marriage, I supported my family as caretaker and nurturer while my husband provided the income as a corporate executive. He often traveled three to five days a week. My mother supported her family in a similar manner while my father earned the family income as a traveling salesman. I often asked her how she handled everything assuming that she felt the same frustrations that I did.

The following is a composite of answers she offered me during those years.
Dear Gloria:

I waited to write because I needed time to think through my answer. It bothers me because I have nothing to tell you that might give you some immediate relief. This seems to be the kind of advice I give most often, things said to relieve symptoms like an aspirin relieves a headache. And now, after taking that time to consider my answer, I don't have one. There is no pill to make you feel better.

You said you find your role as a mother and a wife of a traveling career executive completely exhausting most of the time. You have no energy left during the day or at night to do your writing. You wonder how I handled all I did under similar circumstances with the additional burden of two more children. You are comparing our lives because we accepted similar roles after marriage. But Gloria, you are forgetting you and I are two different women.

My marriage was my happiness, security, and sense of being. It was my identity. My formal education ended in the eleventh grade. I learned nothing academically beyond what I read in novels, and those women and their lives were only stories to me, and living like them was not an option. I sought nothing more because my education and life had taught me not to question, but only to accept and to be thankful for what I had. I relished the quiet hours of naptime and bedtime with my books and a much-needed rest. This was the way it was supposed to be for me. It was not expected by anyone that I should be doing more, especially for myself.

I longed only for the day when you and the boys would be old enough so I could travel with your Dad. That was our dream, to pack my suitcase along with his on Monday and go. Even if it was just down a country road together, at least we wouldn't be saying hello and good-bye so often.

But, Gloria, you had so many options from the time you were a teenager and up through the present that are completely beyond my realm of comprehension. You finished high school and attended college. Your voice was always heard starting with your diary as a little girl, your work on the school newspaper, and all the classes in college and beyond. You never stopped exposing yourself to new and different experiences. You never seem to have enough, and you always see more out there that you want. Your books are not just about other people's lives, they are options for your life and your education makes those options a reality.

I endured much anguish bearing and raising four children alone most of the time, but the pain of physical exhaustion cannot be weighed against what you must experience in mental anguish by stifling your talent in order to be a mother and homemaker. I do hope you only measure yourself against your own standards. And it's not that I consider them too high, or that I think you do, but that they are just there. You are a mother and a wife.

So, to answer your question, how did I endure those years? I just did because it was my job, it was the only thing I did. It was not one I wanted to leave because there was nothing else I wanted to do. I did not have to relinquish one part of me so the other part survived. It was all I wanted because it was all I had.

As to how you can make things better for yourself, I am at a total loss for words. I don't know what it is like to have a poem in my head and not have the energy to put it down on paper. I do know one thing. The way to be the best mother and homemaker is to be happy. And if being happy means spending less time with your family, then do it. The time away from them will give you the strength you need to be the mother and homemaker you want to be—that I do believe! Measure your family time on your scale, not society's.

I will venture one bit of unsolicited advice. Remember what I said about the only thing I dreamed of was traveling with your father? Well, as you know that time never came. Dad's death right after Gordon's graduation was a mockery to me. That fall it was all going to begin! Oh, the trips we planned! But it never happened. And, Gloria, you never know when it will end, this life you share with your husband. So if you value and enjoy it, then go with him when you can.

Don't wait for the perfect time to be together as you once were before the boys were born because that time may never come. Leave the boys with me or friends or hire someone and go. It's good for them at times to see that there are others more important than they are. And God knows it is important that Ed knows you think him significant enough to spend time alone with him. So, please, go enjoy your time as a couple.

There is not much advice here, but maybe what there is will help in some way. One thing you must remember is I will always love you dearly regardless of where you are or what you're doing. Even if all I can offer is something to make you feel better for the moment, I am here and please always know that.

I love you.
Mom

*T*he Value of Play

Joannie Thorsteinson
Calgary, Alberta, Canada

Blessed and cursed with a vivid imagination, I can empathize with my children's need for play, and their need to play with me. I can be a child for a few minutes a day while we build a block tower, dress a doll, or draw something silly. I can do this now, but it took me a while to get here. My journey into play began about two years ago when I first imagined old age.

I envisioned a woman living in an elder-care facility. The arthritis she'd endured since her late twenties now forced her to use a cane and walker to get around. Her fumbling, twisted fingers worked slowly; she could not do up buttons or zippers by herself. This created a humiliating need for assistance in dressing. Perhaps the most embarrassing indignity of her advancing age was her growing incontinence. Relegated to adult diapers, she had lost the battle with the bathroom some years before.

Her children were now successful adults with children of their own. Yet, life in the old folks' residence was routine, boring for her. She desperately wanted to go out for dinner, visit her family in their homes, and have family picnics. She had hoped to do all of these things with her children when they were old enough to appreciate her. Even a little walk in the park would do! They were old enough now, it seemed, and she couldn't understand why they didn't come to take her out.

One day she overheard her daughter discussing her "condition" with a staff member. "She's just so much work," the daughter explained. "She needs help getting dressed, she walks very slowly, and she doesn't always understand what we're talking about, so everything has to be explained to her. She yells when she's

angry or isn't included in things. She's just like a child. It's just too much to expect us to revolve our lives around her!"

The old woman shook with rage and humiliation. She didn't want to be treated like a child, much less described as one. In that moment came a truth. She, herself, had treated her children like children. No, worse than that, she'd treated them like baggage! Now the tables were turned.

I shudder to think of becoming that imaginary old lady. However, the realization that her children were treating her exactly as she'd treated them came clearly to mind. It wasn't just a case of lack of respect or impatience with the old woman's limitations. The missing ingredient was not a lack of gratitude or duty, it was the inability to play!

Yes, play! My son began to teach me how to play one summer morning when he woke me up to watch the sun rise. He was barely five years old at the time. Deftly slipping his small hand in mine, Nikolas explained to me how he saw the gorgeous pinks, oranges, and fiery golds of the natural display. In awe we stood there, looking over the rooftops. He squeezed my hand and sighed, "Mommy, I love you."

My daughter Dannika taught me to play when she began her collection of sticks and branches while we walked her brother to school. She wanted to keep them, so we chose a small vase and gradually filled it with branches and sticks of every description. Every addition brought a memory with it: one stick symbolized the day we saw the rabbit run across the road, another reminded us of the first day we said goodbye to her brother at school. One large branch marked the day we met a little boy at the park. All those days, all those branches, all that play!

I've learned something else, too. Play isn't just relegated to children's games and toys. I looked up the definition of play in the dictionary. The definition I like most is "to amuse oneself." In years past, a pattern of obligation and work overcame my sense of fun and I definitely did not amuse myself. In fact, I felt stretched and strained beyond any reasonable limits. There was always an important chore to do. The floor was dirty, the laundry needed folding. Then there were the surprises my children would spring just before lunch or breakfast. Raspberry jam on the bathroom walls! Oh no…what was that on the carpet… food coloring? Yes, it was, and no, it didn't come out.

I discovered two important truths about play. First of all, children have a natural proclivity to "amuse oneself" and if there are two of them, they often find ways to amuse each other. The food coloring on the carpet was one example of play; my children decorated the carpet. Two years ago I would have gone ballistic over the irreversible stains on the carpet. My husband would have been angry for days. This year, we called the carpet cleaners in, did what we could and moved an area rug to cover the splotches of blue, green, and pink. The area rug looks better there anyway.

I know this explanation sounds so easy-going and liberal that it's hard to believe. Well, I am impressed by the change in my attitude and the way I'm about to relate the positive aspects of the situation. First of all, my children did a lot together that day, without fighting! They even took a bath together to soak some of the food coloring off their multi-colored bodies. Second of all, nothing is irrevocable. The carpet can be tinted back later. Third of all, I learned that nothing in this house can be put high enough to keep it out of Dannika's reach. The fourth and most important lesson is that my two curious children had exhilarating fun together, a memory that will last them (and their parents) a lifetime.

Since I'm writing about play, I feel it's essential to include the most important aspect of play: familial play. More than just amusing the family, familial play undergirds the great celebrations and monumental events of family life. While my family of origin played a bit, and my husband's family of origin didn't play at all, I know familial play exists because I've seen it.

I'm learning to watch my friends who play as a family to see what it is that makes their family events fun. Lots of humor, a little snack, and most importantly,

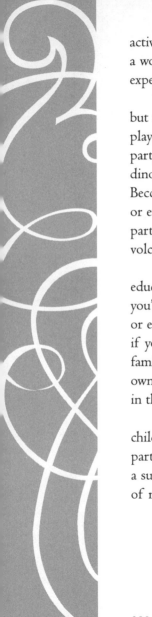

activities that even the adults can enjoy with the children. The event gives everyone a wonderful sense of adventure! As my children proved with their food coloring experience, all people have a sense of adventure.

The second thing that makes family time play time is not only the inclusion, but the active participation of the adults. At Becca's second birthday party, her playful grandmother encouraged all of us to make volcanoes in honor of the party's dinosaur theme. She made dinosaur feet sandwiches, wiggly finger Jell-O dinosaurs, and expected everyone to indulge. I was envious of the creativity of Becca's grandmother, until I realized it wasn't the food or the cake or the Jell-O, or even the volcanoes, that made the party fun for the children. It was the active participation of their parents, and the wonderful adventure we all shared as the volcanoes bubbled over with fake lava!

According to various experts in the field of play therapy, a growing field of educational intervention, familial play has not been extensively researched. So if you're off to the library to find out more on the value of play in adults or family or even how to enhance it in your children, prepare for disappointment. However, if you want to find out more about familial play, share a family celebration with a family who plays a lot. If you can't find a playful family to observe, create your own. You can do this the way I'm learning to, by watching and joining my children in their ever inquisitive need for amusement.

I would ask you to remember my imaginary old woman the next time your child does something just for fun. I'll bet my imaginary friend would love to be a part of something that's just for fun with her children. Also, if you happen to see a sunrise or begin a collection of smelly old sticks in your house, will you think of me? I'm the mother who's learning to play.

Now We Lay Us Down to Sleep

Angela Flom
Burnsville, Minnesota

Along with a new baby comes every piece of advice known to mankind. From which diaper to use to how and when to feed your adorable bundle, I've heard it all. At first I listened attentively to the advice. I was so wet behind the ears. As time went on, though, I learned to read the signs my children gave me. (After all, aren't they the foremost baby experts?) It eventually became quite easy to ignore most self-proclaimed experts. I remember a time when I received top-notch, indisputable, iron-clad advice from a friend.

"Angi, whatever you do, don't rock your babies to sleep all the time. Lay them down even if they fuss. And no matter how unbearable it gets, never, ever lie down with them. Once you start, you'll never be able to stop. Trust me." My boys were difficult to put to sleep, so I figured I should at least give what she said some thought.

After a few weeks, I realized that Tyler's sleeping preferences were not the problem...it was mine. I was the one who loved to cuddle him and rock him to sleep. It wasn't so much that he insisted or that he made my life miserable if I couldn't rock him. It was me, I was the guilty party. Many times I would rock him through his whole nap. Somehow the bathrooms, no matter how dirty they were, never seemed to call loudly enough.

When he got a little older, we were more comfortable on the bed. So we would lie down together for story time and a nap. And as usual, Tyler always had more questions than I had answers.

"Mommy, I know you don't know...but what do you think it is...just what do you think it could be?" became the question of the day. He wasn't satisfied

until I gave him an answer. Funny thing was, it didn't matter whether my answer was right or wrong, as long as it was an answer he approved of. And, of course, as we learn all too quickly, never debate with a two-year-old, for defeat is inevitable.

When our second son was born I was told, "Now Angi, this will be the perfect time to cut out this lying down business. Tell Tyler he's too old for it and for goodness sake, don't start it with Travis."

Well, with only a few slight modifications I was back in business again. We changed afternoon nap-time from 12:30 to 1:00 to fit Travis' schedule and, of course, moved to a bigger bed.

Three years later, nap time is over, but bed time still lingers on. I still wouldn't trade it for all the lottery winnings in the world. You see, many wonderful memories were created there.

One memory that will live forever is of Elliott the Firedog. Elliott moved into our house every night as I told my boys of adventure and friendship. Each tale featured something the boys did that day, whether it was positive or negative. Storytelling became a way of teaching without preaching and without accusing. It was much easier for my boys to learn a lesson from Elliott—after all, he was cool...I was not. It was really quite comical to hear my boys scold Elliott for something they, too, were guilty of. Amazing how kids love to hear about themselves. Sometimes I would try to change the facts, only to get busted each time by the true authors.

As my boys grew older, they told me Elliott stories, which involved me and my parenting skills. They were more helpful than any book I read or nifty advice I received.

Next, we advanced to the progressive Elliott storytelling. I would give the first line, Tyler would say the next, and Travis would sputter out after that, and so on. This became a surefire way to go to bed happy. Each story was such a stitch. They never made sense and Travis usually just repeated what I had already said, but that was the beauty of it.

Another redeeming quality of lying down together is to clear the air. Enforcing discipline is one of the most difficult things to do. So when we lay down, it gave everyone a chance to calmly state his case. Calmly is the key word here. Being Italian, it is very easy to assert my heritage. I can be very hot-headed. So it was no surprise to me that it was passed to the next generation. So calmly now…calmly.

Sometimes things didn't change, but at least we could understand where everyone was coming from. It was a time for everyone to say "sorry" and "thank-you."

It's my goal to make sure that the communication is always flowing, so they have to know that I'm human, too, that I make mistakes just as they do. I also want to make it clear that their opinions count.

Tyler is five and Travis is three now, and we are starting a new phase in our lives. They both start school in the fall, so my husband and I have decided to end our nighttime bed assignments. Although I know we will all be crying ourselves to sleep for a few nights, I also know that the boys need to get to sleep earlier so they can get up earlier. Waking up on the right side of the bed definitely has its advantages.

I think we already set the foundation for open communication. They know we're not going to jump all over them for expressing how they feel, no matter what time it is. Elliott is welcome to stay, he'll just have to pay a visit some other time during the day. As for the cuddling…well, that's a twenty-four-hour-a-day requirement in our house, so that shouldn't be a problem.

$\mathcal{B}$ lended, Extended Family

Susan Wallace Mangas
Miami, Florida

They hadn't really gotten used to the idea of having a stepmother when my husband's children learned I was pregnant. The reception from Silvia, eleven, and Papo, eight, was, well, less than warm.

I suspect their perception of a "step-monster" was as purveyor of poison apples, and as producer of bratty, spoiled, over-indulged half-siblings. With that in mind, my husband Mario and I were absolutely committed to blending this family, not starting another one, and we knew we had our work cut out for us the moment we saw the big red "+" on the home pregnancy test.

We have visitation with the kids every other weekend and a few nights during the week, and we felt it was crucial to include Silvia and Papo in the development of their younger sibling. For starters we bought a great illustrated book, *A Child Is Born*, so the kids could follow the baby's growth and learn as I learned. My stepson was particularly curious about when the fetus was able to hear. The book helped us pin that down and that's when Papo started talking to my belly!

We shared the videotape of the first ultrasound with the kids. They were able to see the baby, and thanks to a quick anatomy lesson, know it was a boy. Slowly but surely this baby thing seemed more real and more "cool!"

It was about that time that we started tossing names around. "Michael" seemed pretty great to me and my husband, but when we ran it past the kids my stepson broke into a fake gagging spell, my stepdaughter huffed and puffed (as only preteens can do) and both announced they would call the baby by ANY OTHER NAME.

Alright, alright, we got the message. So instead of duking it out with them, we asked each of the kids to submit a top ten list of great little brother names. "Alex" was nominated, seconded, and passed by our committee of four!

Throughout the pregnancy, we continually reassured Papo and Silvia of their importance in our family in an effort to keep them from feeling threatened by the baby. We encouraged involvement in their regular activities (cheerleading, baseball, friends) and arranged to have help when the baby was born. That way, we could spend time together as a family doing whatever the older kids wanted to do. (Although we have managed so far to stall my stepson's request to go turtle-catching!)

As the baby grew and began kicking, we talked to the kids about the special role they would play in this little boy's life. How he would probably always think they are so hip and great and funny…how he would be sad when they go to school without him, or leave to go to their mother's house, and how he would bug them to play even when they didn't want anything to do with a little kid!

Silvia and Papo were not on a scheduled visit when the big day arrived and we weren't sure they should be there anyway. So to include them in this important part of the process, and let them feel as though they were somehow front row, we took along two white T-shirts and handed them off to the labor nurse. When Alex finally surfaced, the nurse put his footprints on the official record, then unofficially stamped another set on each T-shirt. They made great gifts when the kids came to meet their baby brother the next day.

When we brought the baby home, we also brought Silvia and Papo with us for a "quiet" family weekend of "get-to-know-the-baby!" It was rough. Nobody slept, but it was a great beginning. The kids got to spend extended time with Alex, talking to and staring at the baby they had seen growing for nine months. They fought over who would help me bathe him, and as I breast-fed, they argued over who got to burp him.

As Alex got older and started to recognize Silvia and Papo, his eyes lit up whenever they came through the front door. They were growing on him and vice versa.

Alex is now five months old and things continue to get better. There are still times when my stepkids need more attention from their Dad or me, and usually after some nudging or a tantrum they admit it. When this happens we do something about it immediately, rather than let the feelings simmer and boil into resentment directed at the baby.

It hasn't been easy. There are days when I think this family could easily come unglued. But on this particular day, it's working and I say a prayer.

A Book of Your Life

Susan Holtzmann Johnson
Mounds View, Minnesota

First tooth. First steps. "Ma-ma" and "Da-da." Important milestones. I kept a record of most of these in a baby book for my daughter. In fact, I had one of those baby books that actually provided you with a calendar and a sheet of stickers so that all you had to do was put the little sticker on the corresponding day. I was filling it in, feeling pretty proud of myself, until one day I was reading through some stickers I hadn't noticed. "First hands." "Focuses eyes." "Turns to sound." I felt incredibly guilty because my daughter was five months old and I had no clue when any of those things happened. Happily, she's now four years old and does all of those things very well in spite of the fact that I didn't record when she started.

My point is, if you were able to read a book about your life, is that what you'd be looking for? Not me. I'd love to know things like: what did my parents think the first time they saw me? What was it like to live through World War II? Did my Dad carry me on his shoulders the way my husband does our daughter? What kinds of ways did I make them happy? How did they deal with all the difficult things they experienced? My parents will probably never publish their memoirs, but their story is invaluable to my siblings and me.

So that is the kind of book I am writing for my daughter. I have a blank journal I bought when I found out I was pregnant. The entries are sporadic and sometimes only a few lines, not even neatly written. But they're a record of my heart and hers, and even though she's only four years old, already there are things I might not even have remembered at all. I wrote about all the things her Dad and I

felt about her in her first few days. I often write about how she has changed our lives and taught us so much. I even wrote about how I ended up shutting myself in the bathroom and crying on a particularly trying two-year-old day.

I'm not a particularly disciplined person, and you don't have to be either. All it takes is your heart and a little spare time. One thing I found helpful is to keep your journal accessible. You'll never do it if you have to dig it out of some box. Mine is by my nightstand. Keep it simple. Don't analyze too much. Try writing as though you were talking to your grown child. Have some scheduled times that you are naturally thinking about them. I always make an entry on my daughter's birthday. It's never too early or too late to start. Anything you can share with your children will be valuable in their eyes.

There are a lot of things I want for my children, but my love is ultimately the only one I'm in control of. As I become a mother of two, I'm sure the "firsts" may be even less adequately recorded. But at least when their Dad and I can no longer sneak into their rooms at night for one last kiss good night, I can read about how we once did.

Everything is Okay!

Vivian Huff
Winston-Salem, North Carolina

For the umpteenth time, my husband is holding our daughter in his arms, consoling her.

"Everything is okay!" " It's alright!" "Sometimes things happen!" "Don't worry, everything will be alright."

Our daughter is twenty-three years old. She's been married for two months. She has just backed her car into the family vehicle!

I could tell young mothers that once your baby birds fly the coop, you and your husband will shout, "Free at last!" Sorry, it won't happen, or to borrow a phrase from today's youth, "Not!"

Your children will always be there, sometimes depending on you, sometimes you depending on them. To make it happen, love them each day. Remember, each is a person in his or her own right. Because they decide to do, say, or act differently than you would does not mean they don't respect, love, and need you.

Stand strong, be their example, their conscience, their devil's advocate. When you make mistakes, admit you've made them so your children will know that you are not perfect and it's okay for them not to be perfect.

Twenty-three years ago, when God placed her in our arms we knew that "Everything was fine. Everything was okay."

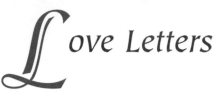ove Letters

Janet Terban Morris
Westport, Connecticut

I began writing letters to my daughter when she was six months old. I had a beautiful fabric-covered journal that I planned to write in while I was pregnant. Being somewhat superstitious, I never did. During her first six months, there never seemed to be enough time or energy to think, never mind write. But midway through her first year, everything seemed to fall into place. We would go for a drive, Sarah would fall asleep, and I would head for the beach. As I filled my head with the scenery and smells of Long Island Sound, my love letters began pouring from my heart to those pages.

I told her I was writing these letters at my most favorite, peaceful place. The smell of sand and salt, sunlight dancing on the water, and her constant breathing in my ear was perfect. The beach was my spiritual place and I wanted her to know that.

Next, I wrote about myself, her Dad, and how we met. I gave her the addresses of places we lived, thinking someday she might like to visit them. I told her about her relatives, her heritage, where she came from, and of what she was made. She was born into a family filled with a great deal of love.

In detail, I discussed my infertility problems, and the doctors, procedures, and surgeries preceding her arrival, letting her know how much she was wanted.

There was always so much to say, I found myself writing almost every day, detailing Sarah's activities and milestones.

The more I got into the practice, the more philosophical I became. Not only was I recounting Sarah's days, I began to talk about myself. I let down my guard and divulged some of my innermost feelings. I began to talk about my dreams, the ones that never materialized, the ones I still hold on to, and especially the ones I have for her. I decided to admit failures, so that she could learn from my mistakes and more importantly, learn to bounce back from misfortune.

In every letter I told her how much I loved her. I wanted her always to know about our closeness, how we laughed and played all day; how we spent so much time together, learning from each other, how we ended our days holding each other.

Every letter was an emotional affirmation of the bond between this mother and her child. I wanted to remember each special moment; the first time she hugged me and I felt she loved me as much as I loved her. My recording it was one way for Sarah to remember it, too.

At one point, I wondered why I had such a need put everything in writing. Was this some kind of fear of my mortality? Was I really afraid that some horrible fate awaited me that would remove me from my child's life? Did I need to make sure Sarah knew how much she was loved, long after I was gone?

Well, maybe in part, but I think the real reason is that as time passes and children grow, we never seem to have as much time to say all the things that are truly in our hearts. Days blend together, dates are forgotten, and yesterday's warm feelings are overshadowed by today's arguments.

Sarah is now five years old. The days of writing to her every day are long gone. Daily entries became weekly. When Jonathan was born, Sarah's letters became less frequent. I have two journals to keep. Once every couple of weeks, I write letters to both of them. Someday, when they are older, I'll turn these diaries of their lives, of our lives, over to them. I hope they will share them with each other because there are different memories in each.

Although I love my children more each day, as they grow and our lives become more complicated, there seems to be less time to tell them. I look at them and marvel at how close we are now. I wonder about the future—their teenage years. Will they be turbulent, defiant times? Will my babies look at me as old, or "square," or "out-of-it?" Maybe during these times I'll give my children their letters.

 As Time Goes By 233

I hope the pure expressions of my love for them will help to bridge the gap. Hopefully, we'll be spared that scenario and the letters will be wedding gifts or something to save for their children. Maybe they will be the boost they need if an insecure time should befall them. Perhaps knowing they were (and are) so unconditionally loved will give them the utmost confidence to succeed at anything they attempt. If nothing else, they are wonderful memories that are theirs to keep.

Acknowledgments

There was a time when this book was simply an idea and there are so many people I need to thank.

First of all, to Tsitsi Wakhisi, my friend, mentor, and main professor at the Graduate School of Communication at the University of Miami, for teaching me everything I know and was able to put into practice to make this book a reality. To my fellow graduate students, Ivy, Kimberly, Megan, Laura, Jackie, Debra, and Roxanne, for all we taught each other that year. To my friend, Selma Edelman, for her friendship, her professional opinion and her unwavering support of my ability.

I also would like to thank literary agents William Clark of the William Morris Agency, Inc., and Janell Walden Agyeman of Marie Brown Associates Literary Services, who very early on graciously agreed to read my manuscript and who provided me with invaluable advice that helped shape and strengthen this book.

Thank you to the eight hundred mothers who mailed their stories to me. I wish I could have used them all. And to the mothers whose stories appear in this book and who patiently waited a year longer than expected to see their work in print because of the car accident: your love and support, one mother to another in my time of great need, let me know that I wasn't alone.

I want to thank my friends Megan Northland, Terri Webber, and Ann de las Pozas for the loving way they have chosen to make this mothering journey with me. To Donna Urban, a courageous woman and mother who made the decision to get involved and who administered life-saving CPR to my daughter. Your face will be forever reflected in every hope and dream we have for Carly.

To my father for teaching me that quitting is never really an option, and that widom and grace are often the same thing.

To my sisters, Michele and Cari, and my brother Marc, for a lifetime of happy childhood memories from 9 Andrea Court, and for our friendships that continue to rise above our loss.

As a writer, I want to thank my high school English teacher, Peter Skilleter, for recognizing in me more than I had yet seen in myself and for helping me find my voice.

To publisher Deborah Werksman, for supporting me not only as a writer and editor, but more importantly as a mother. And to editor Lysbeth Guillorn for her dedication to the quality of this book.

To Ralph Dyer, my husband of ten years, my best friend, and the father of my girls. Your dedication to us as a family has made this book, and the wonderful life we have together, possible.

About the Editor

Traci Dyer received her master's degree in print journalism from the University of Miami in Coral Gables, Florida. She currently resides in Florida with her husband and two daughters.

Join the Conversation!

You are invited to share your unique way of seeing and expressing motherhood by contributing to:

- Mother Voices II: More about the Experience of Motherhood

- Mother Voices III: Mothers of Children with Special Needs
  Write about the Experience of Motherhood

To be considered, please send your submission to:
Traci Dyer/Mother Voices Sequels
c/o Sourcebooks, Inc.
P.O. Box 372
Naperville, IL 60566

Include your full name, address, and phone number. All submissions will be considered for publication. No essays will be printed without written consent. Please do not send original materials, as they cannot be returned. Mothers all over the world are encouraged to submit their experiences so please share this information with a friend.